European Recipes For American Fish & Game

By David Backus

EUROPEAN RECIPES FOR AMERICAN FISH & GAME
Copyright © 1978 by David Backus
Published by Willow Creek Press
P.O. Box 2266, Oshkosh, WI 54903

ISBN - 0-932558-09-7

Dedicated to the proposition
that wild game is a delicacy and
should be prepared that way!

Table of Contents

Introduction

This is a book of simple recipes and procedures based on juxtapositions of native game and fresh fruits and vegetables from woods and garden. Our model is bourgeoise Western Europe - not grand cuisine but loving wholesome celebration of pure products fairly harvested.

We give general procedures. Good cooks use nose, tongue and intuition rather than methodical prescriptions. Imagination is the best spice.

We do not try to hide or mask flavors with elaborate spices and sauces, exotic seasonings and such. Basics neatly coordinated are the basis of real cooking. Use of high quality milk, eggs, butter, wine and spices goes without saying. All substitution detracts, after all. Economy in quality is always, everlastingly false.

We commend use of little salt. All meat and cheese and many vegetables are rich in salt. Added in cooking it often kills more flavor than it enhances. Americans use altogether too much salt, and it can always be made available at table for those who wish it. Like watering a great wine, oversalting at the table insults host and palate. Avoid it, at least until tasting!

Our thoughts come from personal experience and observation at home and in travelling. My personal preference is country cooking from old Provence and the midi of France in general. Reinterpreting this and other European idylls in terms of our superb midwest game and fish has been a jolly pastime.

If this haphazard collection of gastronomic souvenirs brings a small part of the joy of experimentation and discovery to others that its collecting has brought us, we shall indeed be richly paid.

1

THOUGHTS ON TOOLS

Delicate foods carefully handled - this implies certain tools of the trade. Not complex, just the reverse. A country kitchen has all of them except perhaps the blender which is too convenient to pass by: worthwhile progress!

WOODEN FORKS, SPOONS, SPATULAS - infinitely superior to metal which punctures and shreds fish or delicate vegetables. A few very good, very sharp, **BONING KNIVES.**

STEAMER - just a coverable collender that will suspend vegetables above, not in, cooking water - essential to keep flavor and nutrition.

DOUBLE BOILER *(bain-marie)* - to cook gently or hold hot delicate sauce or soup or any food without danger of burning - glass is preferable if flame and oven proof. One good **CHOPPING KNIFE** *(sabatier)* if possible.

BLENDER or **FOOD PROCESSOR** - for fast purees - fast and fool proof.

All glass or all flame and oven proof kitchen ware in ceramic is a cooks dream: inert for acid marinades, easy to clean, versatile, incapable of holding fat or flavors or contributing metallic flavor. One important exception - one or two heavy cast iron skillets for sauteeing. Remember to "season" carefully when new, and never to wash with soap and water: wipe dry, in rare cases boil clean with clear water and a dash of lemon juice.

2

SMALL GAME

MEMORIES OF THE OLD COUNTRY BREAKFAST

How I recall them, breakfasts before the pheasant hunt in brown black Fond du Lac county fields gilded by the red of a rising November sun! Suspended between times and eras, seasons and memories - the great war was over, fathers, sons and griefs had all come home. The subtle treacheries of the cold war were not yet on our minds. To go back, to recapture lost time, repair wounded memories, all in the glow of autumn glory with woodsmoke, the savor of old leather, long idle Winchesters, green corrugated paper shot shells, a tide of bittersweet memory floods and tugs at the heart. Years, miles, oceans, adventures - none has dimmed it.

Cars with black painted hub caps and wood bumpers, relics of chrome rationed 1942 models, still haunted farmyards, the first green, yellow and orange streamliners crisscrossed dairyland, forgetful of encroaching concrete ribbons and the lockheed constellation and the legacy she would leave a burgeoning descendent family. It was all a brief sentimental return, catching wind emotionally; nothing would ever be the same. But it was a grand time to grow up, to educate young emotions.

We'd be up just before dawn and already the kitchen fire would be high, coffee simmering, a pot of glistening burnished maple syrup gently warming on the wood range, straight from our cousins' sugarbush in then far and wild Price county.

A boiling pot of water was ready for generous slabs of salt pork from which most of the fat would be boiled out by the time I got down stairs to watch my elders. These parboiled chunks were thoroughly dredged in flour and fried slowly in a big dusty black iron skillet. The smell, mixing with syrup and coffee - oh, description pales! When the pork was crisply golden brown fresh cream flooded the skillet and the pork was served smothered in this thick sauce. Thick buttermilk pancakes baked in another skillet and always these were accompanied by sunny side up eggs in which a bit of ground tarragon was cast before they set up. Only fresh butter in these skillets, needless to say, sweet, home churned still, a straw yellow entirely different from store spreads.

Even as we ate, my aunt would be mixing dried peas into the water that had parboiled the salt pork - peas, onions and even a big ball of garlic - rare enough in northern European bred families. We would have rich pea soup before our pheasant course that evening.

Big fluffy slices of home made bread toasted on the grill of the oven. These would make a brief call in the egg frying butter before being piled on a hot plate in mid table. Yesterday's leftover pheasant floured and crisped in the salt pork pan with the addition of a bit more butter - a delicate and almost complex mix of flavor - pork, butter, a bit of creamy residue, and fresh pheasant, flaky and rich with that certain friendly wildness that tickles the back of the mouth.

The long days in the corn, the brushy rose twined hedgerows, bronze bombs launching from cattails still root captured in floating ice, sparkling with crystalline dawn light, all wonderful souvenirs. Blase', burdened memories still respond, however, to those smells and sounds of home, of farmhouse breakfasts, perhaps because they are so contained and personal. I still make breakfast with vivid tugs of these visions, smells and savors. The salt pork procedure cannot be improved - ambrosia! And butter fried pheasant with eggs, pancakes and real maple syrup is still a combination fit for kings. My aunt always had a big bowl of apples, red and huge, in the middle of the breakfast table. Pockets would bulge with them as the men left for the first drive of the day, shells in one pocket, apples in another, Winchesters over work muscled shoulders.

We youngsters used to split a few of those apples, dip them in maple syrup and butter and roast them over the range coals on long forks. Auntie showed us how and founded a tradition. If you want a superb after breakfast sweet by the campfire, look no further.

L' OMELETTE a l'ABRUZZES (FRITTATINE)

This rich liver and cheese omelette is a superb use for livers of game birds; so prepared they are more appreciated than in conventional stuffings.

Saute livers of grouse and pheasant, woodcock or all other wild fowl in butter with finely chopped onion, garlic, salt, pepper, a trace of oregano and chopped parsley. Chop the cooked liver into fine cubes, and keep warm in the cooking pan.

Make a rich omelette mix of eggs and heavy cream with 2 yolks for each egg white, with enough melted butter to facilitate cooking in very lightly greased skillets. Beat until creamy, put a thin layer in the pan and, when almost done, spread liver, onion and garlic and pan drippings from cooking these, on the still undone top of the omelette, staying in from the edges. Roll each omelette into a loose cylinder and finish in the oven with a generous coating of grated romano cheese on top of each rolled omelette.

These may be served as finished in the oven or with an added tomato sauce made by stewing together fresh diced tomatoes, chopped onion, garlic, green peppers and celery in equal parts. This sauce should be simmered for a long time and should be finished and held hot before starting the omelettes themselves.

Alternatively one may add liver to omelette still earlier in its progress, put the grated parmesan cheese on top of the liver, *inside* the rolled omelette. In this case allow more oven time to thoroughly melt and blend cheese inside the roll. In either case, a moderate (325 - 350 degrees) is to be desired - never hotter.

If tomato sauce is not used, garnish with paprika and fresh chopped parsley.

CREAMED CHIPPED SQUIRREL

For this preparation choose young tender greys, clean and wash immediately and bone, cutting meat into rather thin wedges and chips and slivers.

Dredge thoroughly in flour, pepper, oregano, thyme, sage, and very *little* salt or better none.

Saute gently in plenty of fresh butter until meat is golden browned and almost done - not too long. Add finally a cup of diced raw turnip for each two squirrels - or even a bit more if you want to stretch. When the turnips start to be tender over low heat, mix in heavy cream and beaten egg yolks, 2 yolks per cup of cream, to make a thick, creamy, and uniform mix. Into the oven, tightly covered, cook slowly for an hour or more until everything is very tender. About 15 minutes before serving lace with good plain brandy, mix thoroughly, and heat piping hot for the table. Serve dipped over freshly grilled, crisp French bread in shallow soup plates, garnish with chopped parsley.

POTTED SQUIRREL AND RED CABBAGE

Grey northern squirrel can be prepared with any rabbit recipe. But this is a rather special and regal version.

Hang squirrels after cleaning at near freezing - do not wash! Lightly aged squirrels should then be washed, skinned, cut into serving pieces and just submerged in red wine vinegar for 4 - 6 days, in a glass or crockery pot.

To prepare: in a heavy iron skillet fry chunks of lean hickory cured side pork or bacon, to make a thick flood of fat. Dry the squirrel, flour and pepper it liberally and into the hot skillet with the bacon; fry until gently browned and more than half tender. Add a cup of finely chopped red cabbage per squirrel, ¼ cup fine chopped onion per squirrel, mix and saute together for a minute or two to coat everything with fat and mix bacon chunks evenly, barely submerge in *dark* German beer (bock beer can do), cover and simmer in a medium oven until liquid is almost reduced to nothing . . . perhaps 1½ hours or longer, at 325 degrees or thereabouts.

Sauce: 1 pint thick sour cream; 1 *heaping* tablespoon dry mustard, 1 *scant* teaspoon horseradish (dry, grated) a dash of nutmeg. Blend thoroughly, hold at room temperature to top each serving of the hot ragout, dipped right from the skillet into prewarmed plates or shallow tureens.

Suggested accompaniments: Dark green salad with a sharp garlic dressing, hard rye rolls and tall steins of dark beer or real stout if you can find it. With this we have moved far north of our French hare "ragout" and into the damp dark northern forests and undulating moors of damp salty northern islands.

RABBITS vs HARE

Although he shoots both side by side, cooks and savors both at the same table, the true Frenchman never confuses his lapin (rabbit) and his lievre (hare). Every bag in western Europe is mixed but sportsmen and chefs respect and celebrate the nuances.

The culinary gulf separating our little agricultural belt cottontail and his rangy woods browsing second cousin, the snowshoe hare, is far larger than that between lapin and lievre. A soft young Sauk county cottontail can, as the traditional books tell us, be prepared like a chicken. The Price county hare in February is a different bunny. One looks to the brooding castles of Northern Europe for "rabbit" preparations which fit this bundle of gamey energy, worthy of real care and time. The recipes presented here reflect syntheses of this European tradition for the hare, and a native mid-american approach for our little cottontail, so unique to the hedgerows of dairyland, beloved by boys and men and farmhouse cooks since wagon and ox days. The difference is not glossed here!

RAGOUT OF HARE

Cut cleaned, healthy snowshoe hares into serving pieces of generous size. (As the season progresses and hares grow stronger of savor, hanging in the skin at just over 32 degrees F. vastly improves texture and flavor - but never hang a badly ragged animal - potent argument for killing the snowshoe at close range with fine shot and light loads.)

Grind fresh black pepper corns very fine - just the reverse of usual for gourmet uses! - and rub each piece of hare until quite permeated. Now cover all the serving pieces with red wine vinegar in which you have crushed liberal fresh garlic and onions and some laurel bay leaves. Use a glass or crockery vessel and turn the meat once a day. The marinade process should last about a week, longer for older well hung hares. Ice box temperature is ideal.

The day of cooking, drain the meat dry, pat with a soft cloth and dredge each piece thoroughly with plain flour (rye or dark wheat is much better for flavor than white American bread flour!) Prepare a good iron skillet full of chopped hickory smoked bacon chunks cut from a real slab and brown the hare to golden crispness in a generous bath of fat - moderate heat rather than smoke hot, please. Put hare and bacon and a little of the cooking fat in a stew pot, add an equal sum of coarsely cut turnip, cabbage and fresh carrots; cover with the marinade, seal tightly and let simmer slowly in a slow oven all the day long, slowly reducing temperature as you go, from 350 degrees to about 225 degrees at late afternoon or evening dinner hour. Before serving drain off the liquid and keep the now butter tender meat and vegetables hot in the oven. Thicken the liquid with a bit of flour, you should need no additional seasonings, and pour it piping hot back into the stewpot, which is taken right to the center of the table.

Ideal accompaniments are hard rye rolls and crisp salad of a dark green leaf lettuce with sharp roguefort dressing and a robust burgundy - never bordeaux, please! with vinegar marinated rabbit or hare! - a perfect blend of traditions and preferences such as an Austrian or south German bourgeoise would prepare it today. The further south you go the more likely the cook will put just a whiff of brown sugar in the thickened sauce. But so little you can't believe it! Try it both ways before deciding.

FOX RIVER COTTONTAILS

Use small, tender and very fresh young rabbits early in the year preferably at a time when the last garden corn is still available.

Cut into rather small boneless cubes at least one bunny for each dinner member. Dredge thoroughly in flour lightly seasoned with fresh pepper and a bit of finely rubbed sage - no salt. Fry slowly until brown in a deep skillet of good butter, drain, and put into a tightly covered ovenware casserole to bake very slowly until tender to an ordinary dinner fork. Be sure to cook well done.

Meanwhile steam - don't boil - one ear of corn per person, cut from the cob deeply, remembering that much precious flavor lies in the cob just under the kernels. Into the reheated pan drippings you reserved after frying the rabbit put the cut corn, stir and sizzle lightly until all the kernels are separated, teased, not broken apart, with a fork. Since some flour from frying has remained in the skillet some thickening has already taken place; finish this with an egg you have whipped gently into a bit of heavy cream and add to the skillet to make a creamy rich white sauce around your corn. Pour the entire skillet sauce over the rabbit and let the whole simmer very slowly together while you make up a batch of your very shortest, lightest, fluffiest baking powder biscuits, large caliber.

Each guest should have a deep soup tureen at his place; into this put a steaming fresh from the oven biscuit with a generous chunk of butter in each split half. Over upturned, buttered biscuits ladle your rabbit in creamed corn sauce hot from the casserole. Each may be topped with a generous green top hat of fresh chopped parsley.

This superbly simple farmhouse rabbit is very difficult to equal. Only substandard ingredients - frozen meat, frozen corn, imitation shortening or grocery store commercial biscuits can ruin it, but they will do so exquisitely! Do it correctly, or not at all.

When the tea kettle sang, cedar spit in the stove, and home made cider gleamed amber-gold in grandma's cut glass, this rabbit in creamed corn sauce has a reward for kings, a humble crown for grand times and simple joys.

AUBERGINES AU COG

Carefully hollow out large fresh eggplants leaving a fairly thick layer of skin and flesh. Lightly rub interior with pepper, a trace of salt, thyme, and oregano.

In a skillet with a little butter saute diced white onion, cubed raw grouse, partridge, quail or pheasant meat (perhaps cuttings from a recipe which employed only breasts of these birds. When these are essentially done add cut tops of asparagus and continue cooking only until these are half done. Put sauteed mixture tightly in hollowed eggplants, pour pan drippings in and over, and bake in an open pan until exteriors of egg plants are nicely tender to a dinner fork. Garnish with sprigs of crisp parsley.

Serve with crisp watercress and roguefort salad and white or rose wine.

SALADE AN COG ROGUEFORT

Bake in white wine boned meat of grouse and/or pheasant as available. For best effect use breast meat. Saute livers lightly in butter. When done drain and chill both thoroughly and dice medium coarse. Dust with oregano and thyme, keep refrigerated.

Chop 1 cup each watercress, crisp celery and dark green leaf lettuce; prepare ½ cup each chopped fresh parsley, green onions or shallots, stuffed olives.

To this sum total of about 4½ or 5 cups of greens add 1 generous cup of crumbled Roguefort or Danish bleu cheese, 2 cups of grouse or pheasant meat, about 3/4 cup of chopped livers. Toss altogether in a chilled bowl, adding a bit of freshly ground white pepper - sparingly!

Serve in individual chilled salad bowls lined with lettuce leaves and wedges of tomato, lemon and lime slices for garnish and a tureen and dipper with this simple dressing:

¼ cup olive or corn oil

½ cup white wine vinegar

Bruised and fine chopped fresh garlic plus a whiff or two of dry mustard. (Mix very thoroughly in a blender if available. Dressing should be room temperature).

FONDUE PIEMONTAISE

Hors d' oeuvre and dinner fondues are usually based on light cheese and white wine; this one is gentler and richer, ideal for brunches, even breakfast.

Melt 1 pound of Fontina, Mozzarella or "white" baker's cheese, ¼ pound fresh butter slowly in a double boiler (the bain-Marie so dear to all French cooks and home makers); slowly add three lightly beaten egg yolks mixed with just enough light cream to make a richly light yellow consistency resembling thick egg nog in appearance and consistency. Season lightly with finely rubbed tarragon.

In Italy's piedmont, this "fonduta", topped with thin slices of truffles, is served in an oven proof casserole less as a dip than a superbly sauced truffle preparation. For truffles one can substitute morels or mushrooms sliced and lightly sauteed. For a more substantial dish, top with slices of sauteed grouse or pheasant livers.

But it is effective to use "fonduta" as a hot chafing dish dip for this delicacy:

Bone pheasant breasts whole and beat each slab of meat *gently* with a meat hammer until it is flat and very soft but still holding its shape; do not destroy the meat, flatten it! Rub these large slices of pheasant with flour, working the flour into the meat. Add a little fine paprika or pepper and rubbed sage to the flour if you wish. Saute these gently and individually in a skillet of olive oil for a nuance of flavor. Butter is equally good but the olive oil is a delightful foil in the end product. Fry very crisply, cut carefully into silver dollar sized pieces and dry out in a *slow* oven on a rack so there is no grease at all. These "chips" of pheasant are presented on a hot platter, to be dipped in the chafing dish filled with steaming "fonduta". Exquisite for buffets or a hearty before-hunt breakfast, with crisp French bread, grilled and garlic buttered, and thick slices of grilled Parma ham.

DUCK, PHEASANT OR GROUSE LIVERS TARRAGON

You may even combine the three species if you have a mixed bag. Clean livers carefully, wash, pat dry, dredge in a mixture of flour and a dash of dry mustard - just a tiny dash. In a heavy skillet melt a generous portion of butter, chopped shallots or green onions, and finely rubbed tarragon rather liberally. Then saute the livers, whole, until quite done. Remove, save pan liquid; envelop each liver in a thin supple crust dough and close tightly like a ravioli. Bake on a buttered shallow casserole until golden browned and firm, hollow sounding when "thumped" gently.

Keep livers and pan butter warm; mix thick sour cream with white wine tarragon vinegar, chopped parsley and a touch of rubbed tarragon leaves as well if you want to intensify the flavor. Cover the casserole of crust-wrapped livers with pan butter - they will glisten admirably - top each with a generous spoon of the sour cream, finish to serving warmth in a hot oven - a very few minutes - and present as a luncheon entree or a hearty hors d' oeuvre.

COG FRANCOIS (RUFFED GROUSE, OR EVEN PHEASANT OR PARTRIDGE BREASTS, IN A CRUSTY SHELL).

Melt liberal quantities of fresh sweet butter in a thick pan, saute there minced fresh onions and garlic, and when these are lightly cooked saute there also *boned breasts* of 4 grouse. When birds are tender but not over-cooked, put aside and prepare a supple, rich pate crust which can be rolled very thinly. It will help to include an egg or egg yolk in the crust mixture. Make each piece of grouse breast (usually a half) a generous, loose fitting jacket and seal each tightly. Bake on a greased sheet very slowly until the crusts are flaky and golden brown. Before wrapping each sauteed grouse breast be sure to butter it liberally.

Meanwhile: add a dash or several dashes of tarragon to the pan of butter, onion and garlic, dilute it with ½ bottle of good, but not premium, chablis (or even another *dry* white wine) and reduce it a little over a slow fire. Thicken gently with 2 to 3 yolks and enough thick cream to make a velvety creamy yellow sauce. When the crusted grouse breasts are done, dry, and golden flaky, put on a very hot platter, smother in the sauce, cover with grated parmesan and/or romano cheese, fresh parsley and paprika for color. Serve with chablis or a light rose.

WILD TURKEY CHAMPLAINE

Choose a sizeable gobbler, hang him well, in the feathers, very thoroughly eviscerated. Pluck, wash and pat dry.

Trim all the rind from a large slab of bacon (real hickory smoked deep south lean bacon, please!), cut a pound or even two of the bacon into coarse nuggets. Stuff the turkey tightly with the cut bacon, raw brussel sprouts, raw white pearl onions, and washed raw jumbo mushrooms. This will not expand, stuff *very tightly*. Envelop the bird as much as possible with the bacon rind, pin with skewers to hold it in place over the breast especially. Roast uncovered but *very slowly* until butter tender, basting with drippings particularly those parts not totally covered by the bacon rind.

Make a rich gravy of the drippings by diluting with a rich red wine and thickening finally with a bit of flour as necessary; add sage, thyme, and oregano as desired.

Bake Louisiana yams in the same oven, open and fork up in the skin, drench the interiors with Vermont maple syrup, and return to the oven until syrup is sizzling and a bit foamy in the potato interior. Top each yam with fresh butter and sprinkle with nutmeg before serving.

Carve the turkey and serve pieces atop the vegetables in the cavity, drenching with the gravy just before serving each plate. Offer the yams kept very hot, on the side, in individual heat proof dishes. Serve with a big Rhone wine, preferably Chateauheuf-du-Pape.

CANARD SAUVAGE COINTREAU (BRANDIED WILD DUCK)

Wash thoroughly and peel a dozen large oranges and a lemon; retain the peelings and use them to *tightly pack* a well hung wild duck, or two if smaller. To completely pack bird or birds augment peels with chunks of a tart apple, raw of course, and coarsely chopped white onions.

Roast birds with a jacket of thin slices of salt pork, until tender, in a slow oven. (Save drippings for soups or stews.)

Rub the oranges and lemon pulp into a puree and cook until reduced by 1/3 or nearly so. When birds are thoroughly done carve, present quarters or serving pieces over a bed of the stuffing. Bring the orange-lemon puree to a sharp boil, expand quickly with cointreau brand orange brandy to a creamy sauce texture, pour over duck and stuffing on hot platter held in a medium oven.

To accompany: bake Idaho potatoes fluffy dry, mix potato with enough buttermilk or sour thick cream to make a smooth stiff mix, add butter to emptied skins, replace potato mix, lightly sprinkled with nutmeg, more butter atop each refilled potato and return to the oven until ready to serve; at the last moment dust each open restuffed potato with grated romano cheese, paprika and parsley for color and flavor.

A conventional burgundy or beaujoulais is desired for this course.

SALMIS GRAND HOTEL

(This procedure may also be used with old and large wild ducks).

Hang a large wild goose until well aged. Pluck and cut into serving size pieces (wing-back, ¼ of breast, legs, thighs are the usual cuttings) after boning. Reserve carcass, put in large soup pot with cut onions, bay leaf, sage, oregano and other spice to taste; reduce to a rich bouillon over several days, strain coarsely to remove bones and solids.

Meanwhile marinate goose meat 2 - 3 days in red wine, cut onions and a goodly sum (often 2 - 3 whole heads) of garlic, fresh, chopped coarsely. A trace of fresh lemon squeezed in the marinade is lovely.

Before dinner: saute meat lightly in fat with fresh cut onions; bacon fat from diced smoked bacon left in the pan is excellent. When brown and crisp put in tight casserole with marinade liquid, onion and garlic and cook *gently* for several hours until meat is butter tender. Do not peek too much! Use 2/3 of your goose bouillon as liquid to make a platter of wild rice and brown rice mixed. The grains should be dry and never caked. All bouillon should be absorbed. Remaining bouillon goes into the casserole and all the casserole liquid is thickened into a dark gravy during the last 30 minutes of cooking. Hot fresh rice, crisply separate and flaky, is bedded on a very hot platter, topped with hot goose and casserole gravy which should be quite abundant.

Serve with steamed brussel sprouts put in individual oven proof serving dishes, liberally buttered, a bit of fresh cream, and covered with grated Parmesan cheese, each returned to the oven to melt the cheese around the sprouts and butter cream.

A Rhone of body or a very big Burgundy is needed for this hearty fool proof goose platter. At the club the marinade and the table wine were the same: an elegance scarcely necessary in this age!

SPRING DUCK EPINARDS COINTREAU

This is a "fancy" way to serve frozen ducks from fall, too old for simpler roasting or broiling.

Bone a big duck or a brace; slice breast meat thin, all other chipped into relatively thin pieces. Soak overnight in a crock with one or two crushed oranges, and a sinfully large measure of plain cognac.

In a well buttered casserole put a layer of rhubarb stems cut julienne; a layer of shredded spinach; a layer of duck slices and orange pulp; repeat the sequence; top with spinach leaves, then a thick layer of hickory smoked bacon cut thick. Cover tightly, bake at about 400 degrees for an hour until duck is tender when whole thickness of casserole is pierced with a fork - gently.

Dampen thoroughly with cointreau liqueur just before serving, heat piping to 425 degrees uncovered to crisp bacon, garnish with orange and lime sliced translucent thin, parsley sprigs and mint leaves if you have it in your garden. Suggested accompaniment - tart au gratin potatoes or cauliflower, or fresh native asparagus with lemon butter, and a sparkling burgundy.

PHEASANT CASSEROLE AU GRATIN

Bone one or two large pheasants, keep breasts whole and neat, cut all the remainder of the meat up finely. Slice each half breast to make 4 big thin slices per bird. Pound lightly with a dull meat hammer to flatten, and pound in gently flour to which you've added fine ground pepper, thyme, oregano and sage. Dip floured seasoned slices in egg yolk beaten with a bit of cream and then coat with toasted bread crumbs crushed very fine. (As always use real French bread if you can - dry, crisp, without sugar or fat. Shun grocery store breads not worthy of the name.) Chill very smartly.

Saute all the cut meat in a skillet of butter and diced green onion and on the side steam some heads of cauliflower lightly. In a food blender puree cauliflower and sauteed meat to creamy consistency - pan butter will thin it adequately. Still in the blender add thick sour cream to make a liberal, spoonable sauce - not too much.

Saute cold breaded breasts smartly until golden and done quite tenderly; butter a casserole, half the puree in the bottom, slices of pheasant next, large slices of aged Swiss or Jarlsborg cheese on each piece, balance of puree on top, finally sliced raw tomatoe and a thick layer of grated parmesan and romano cheese. About 45 minutes in a hot (375 degree) oven, covered save for the last 10 - 15, to brown the cheese coat. Chopped parsley or watercress garnish.

AFRICAN STYLE GROUSE

Uncle Bert was a fabulous character - fabulous, I say, in the classical sense: the fables to which his drole personnage gave rise for exceeded the reality of the man. Bert was rich, his Brittanies had magic noses, he never missed a cock or ruff inside forty yards, Bert had world-wide mafia connections to obtain the wines and delicacies he and his wife preferred, he had a mistress in London, in Brussels and in New York - the legend is endless and delightful.

Bert was no one's uncle and almost everyone's good friend. His name was Bertrand, a hard one to carry through school. If well off, he was neither rich nor a libertine in the usual sense, and he did - occasionally - miss a shot at a grouse with one of his exquisite little Darne twenties. Very occasionally!

Among the originals of our Old Tamarack coterie, I recall him best from a few years later, at the club, on winter evenings. The fire would be roaring, a quietly gay crowd circulated in the great reception room, white coated waiters carried simple heavy silver trays of Martinis, green icy clear and frosty, burnished, tawny manhattans, which picked up the golden flood of firelight in a magical kaleidoscope of luminous reflections. Bert's drink was dry French Vermouth on the rocks with a curl of lemon - and Bordeaux with dinner, of course.

Good guns, good dogs, good food, good books - these things summed up Uncle Bert's world - and they were the only things on which he lavished time or money. Otherwise he was spartan: a professor, he was not professorial, and his long sojurns across the ocean were, I think, more often devoted to shooting and talking chase than to the library work for which he went. Perhaps he squeezed the professional activities in with the most important, here and there. I suppose so.

"Dig the hole deeper, boys - deeper yet." There were two of us - I the young greenhorn passionately delighted to spend a weekend with a professor in the field in which my interests were just starting, and doubly so to spend a shooting weekend with a living legend. I owed the favor, I think, to the cancelling out of another guest, but Uncle Bert did like me, and was pleased to tell his anecdotes, literary stories, and favorite theories to avid ears. He had told me a good many at the club.

My shovel mate was one of Bert's graduate students, as I recall. I was surprised at his interests which centered much more on grouse than on academe. I think my continual attempt to probe their literary wisdom was more annoyance than joy to them.

The sun was setting on our Price County swamp rim where Bert's shack (I mean shack) slouched. (Once it may have stood there - at the epoch of my visit, slouch was the word!)

The three of us built a huge bonfire in the 3 foot deep pit Bert had cajoled and directed his crew to dig. We sat about the fire and discussed the hunt for morning. Provisions brought from home gave us, under Bert's direction and practiced hand a most delightful supper: quarters of aged Wisconsin pheasant dipped in spiced oil and lemon juice and roasted on green alder spits over the fire after its fury died a bit, in the green black northwoods dark. The smells, the firelight on the trees, the pheasant perfumed smoke hanging in late October moonlight, in air moist and cuttingly fresh, all was magic.

The next morning's hunt, in black alder and aspen bottoms quite near the cabin, was beyond description. Routine to Bert, the quantity and excitement of the shooting was intoxicating to me. We were in by 11, under a weak sun, with three limits, of which Bert had collected more than his proportion (with fewer shells than I had used, or than his graduate student had used - no need to say!)

"Build up the fire, fellows," Bert called from the cabin. We built an inferno on the evening's coals. Bert was supposed to be cleaning the grouse. He did, but he had six left to which he had done nothing, and oddly these were the best birds - not shot up, almost pristine, huge. I was too wise to ask. The bulk of birds went into a box of ice, fresh bought at Lac du Flambeau the night before and bedded in a box of Milwaukee dry ice - and you can imagine this a most efficient refrigerator! The fire was wasted - Bert tossed a salad for lunch, superb but scarcely rustic. "Not like Andre," he quipped - Andre was the clubs' salad chef, then fresh from Toulouse - "but more honest." This was Bert's favorite phrase for all affectations from recoil pads and stock monograms to aesthetic salads too pretty to attack.

Then the ritual started. Bert himself went down to a preferred spot south of the cabin and hauled back bucket after bucket of wet swamp clay. I thought he was out of his mind but I certainly was not about to ask any stupid questions. My young counterpart took all this calmly. I don't know if he had seen it all before or if the wisdom of having a master's degree gave him more dignity than I.

Bert doused his 6 best grouse with water and rolled them in swamp clay and then in dry red sand in the edge of the fire area. I was right! He was crazy; the old man was simply eccentric, at least!

Then designs began to occur to me. Bert tossed three buckets of charcoal on the ardent maple/alder coals and directed us to cover the whole with a light coat of sand and some green still leafy oak branches. Then the mud balls with whole grouse inside; more sand; ventilation holes punched with long sticks in the edges of the pit of coals. By 2:30 we and the two eager Brittanies were out for woodcock. Bert's poisonous little 28 gauge Darne, his woodcock gun, was as efficient as our canine partners. (No one shot at a grouse all afternoon, of course: one does not mix specialties - not if one is Uncle Bert.) What a pile of cocks we brought in at 6! Bert hung each lovingly from the porch roof with fine wire - save for a few birds mutilated by my "gross" loads (20 gauge number nine skeets!) which were cleaned on the spot. Bert used handloads with number 11 shot. Don't laugh. I don't think I ever saw him miss a timber-doddle!

Dinner that evening was rare.

We dug out the clay coated grouse while Bert made a big salad glistening with olive oil, two kinds of lettuce, big white onions and other good greens thanks to the ice layer box which rode - and stayed - outside in the open end of Berts' immaculate 1946 wood-sided Ford wagon (do you remember that workhorse, now a classic car?!) A bottle of Chateau Trimoulet was open, smoking ancient savor at the center of the plank topped table which dominated the shack. Three big old kerosene lamps made fantastic shadows and the wood stove cast its etherial glow from none too well fitted seams.

The clay balls were Vesuvius - hot, hard as cement. Bert broke them with the wood box hatchet. Feathers came away without taking more than a few patches of skin; the entrails were dried into balls which almost fell out of the birds. A bit of deft knife work dispatched heads and leg joints and Bert presented his birds split rapidly, spread out, doused well with a butter just lightly laced with cool vermouth, fresh ground pepper - just a bit - and that was all. 10 minutes or so out of the fire, piping hot, I can only describe these as "sheer essence of grouse." I had never, and have never since, duplicated it in any other cooking method. It is one, not the only, way to savor our foremost feathered game. If you've not tried it you have missed a treat and a spectacle worthy of many tales.

This is a common cooking method among black Africans in primitive societies, and was discussed - and used - by Osa and Martin Johnson on their pioneering African works of the twenties. The Africans knew far more about enjoying life than the colonists, generally Englishmen who boiled their beef.

The Africans used it on big birds - their turkey sized bustard most commonly. And the French, always so civilized, indeed knew the trick early, for I find several recipes for "poulet bohemienne" which describes basically the same procedure, in several old, revered works on cuisine.

It is not all that simple. Big bath tub sized pits are needed to get big birds done; who cares to dig that much? Little birds are easy to cook too done because enough insulating clay will not stick. Overshot birds will be spoiled by cooking with damaged entrails inside, but eviscerated birds will tend to admit water and clay and ash even if sewed up, and tend to be too dry. Finally, cooking with entrails intact but undamaged is apparently crucial to the concentrated flavor, just like cooking autumn squash with peel on, whole, with seeds inside. Thus, the daintily shot grouse is perfect for this grand celebration.

That night we talked books, and finished two birds apiece, and opened a second bottle of Trimoulet. The salad was a perfect foil, it was a memorable occasion, one among many when Bert was "entertaining."

By rights I should recall the inspiration Bert brought to my literary work, his gentle kindness with a young aspirant to academia, the subtle influence his razor edge tongue and mind always had on me throughout the university. I do.

But I recall the pit baked grouse and that evening in the land of the voyageurs and the Ojibwa even better - the worth of the sport, the ceremony of the meal, and all the rest. When I see the "spaniel ears" on a slender Darne double in some Paris armourer's window, I always think of fastidious Bert, his number 11 shot, and those "African style" grouse. I smell and taste them still. "Grouse a l Africain?" "Gelinotte bohemienne?" Take your choice. For me it will always be just plain "Uncle Bert's partridge." If one be as crazy as Bert - would that we all could be - one might just want to try this. But don't do it without willing and wondering diggers. For the chef this just must be half the fun.

3

TO HANG OR
NOT TO HANG?

The eternal issue - should the woodcock, the duck, the pheasant, hang until they drop from their hanging wire in the kitchen, pantry or on the porch - or should they be cleaned and prepared fresh? Should the grouse ever be hung?

The French - Belgian tradition always *hangs* small game, rather extensively.   Other European cookeries eschew the practice or employ it very sparingly.   Where does age stop and spoilage start? Or does one necessarily follow the other?   What is the best way to savor your hardwon birds?   What is safe as well as savorous?

Traditionally these "ageings" are made on uneviscerated birds. The undamaged bird, supposedly does not putrify, but decomposes from indigenous organisms.   Brillat Savarin, perhaps the greatest of French culinary artists in international reputation, commended hanging "le faisan" until the abdomen turned green!   Grimond de la Reyniere said a pheasant killed at Mardi Gras would be ready to prepare on Easter!   These are not extremes!

A few more contemporary French gastronomes (Curnonski for example, is one) simply advocate using small game fresh with no attempt at ageing of any kind.

All high quality domestic red meat is lightly aged under refrigeration.   Prime beef receives particularly extended ageing, which is an aspect of its flavor you would miss if eaten truly fresh.   No one would eat venison - elk, moose or whitetail - without long ageing in cold, either natural (the woodshed) or artificial (locker plant). All such meat would rapidly spoil at high temperatures since it is thoroughly inoculated by exterior organisms.   Some breakdown of course occurs which tenderizes and flavors the meat.   It is of a totally different sort than that which occurs in European style hanging.

Any furred or feathered game which is primarily red meated (as opposed to white) benefits by low temperature ageing, up to the point where the meat has darkened a bit and perhaps even surface dried slightly. Such ageing does nothing for white-meated birds except dry them out. Only late fall early winter temperatures in the upper midwest permit this "cold-age" out of a refrigerator.

And the other side of the medal:

A perfectly intact bird, not damaged by shot, may be hung "as is" for periods ranging from a few days to a week or more, when odor begins to form, in room temperature, or even outside on a screened, insect-free porch. Europeans usually hang game in the kitchen, though early fall temperature in September (even August) bird seasons in northern France permits porch hanging of intact small game. Presumably *all* decomposition is derived from organisms native to the bird's body; *no* foreign organisms are entered by way of shot wounds, or at least none within the body cavity. The result is a bird properly "hung" (Faisande is the French term, derived from their pheasant - faisan, a bird always fit for table only after hanging, in the culinary tradition) and of a savor uniquely different than fresh or conventionally "aged" birds.

Can you safely practice this "hanging" (as opposed to cold "ageing" of eviscerated game) with our ducks, cocks, pheasants and dark fleshed birds of the grouse family? That depends.

Most American gamebirds are overshot, a result of cannons and gross loads and shot. Such game really should not even be frozen. It spoils rapidly even then. If you hunt, shooting flying, with very light loads and fine shot, and bring home many truly intact birds you are a rarity but you may well try ageing by hanging if you are sure of your ability to be honest about that word "intact." That means the grouse stunned out of the air by a thin cloud of 9 or 10 shot, not riddled with 6 shot as by bullets.

Err on the side of too little, not too much, hanging, until you are sure of your ground. Hanging concentrates and improves *all* feathered game, white or dark. The dark meats - waterfowl, 'cocks, dark grouse - accept and benefit from more than grouse, partridge, quail etc. Doves (if you go south) age gorgeously hung European style. Do not overdo the "room" temperature. Anything over 45 degrees F. will hang game and is slower and more manageable, especially for first attempts.

Never try to hang rabbits, they must all be examined for disease in the field.

You may not like "hung" birds.   Eventually most knowledge-able eaters do. Recall that hung game is almost invariably marinated before cooking. Use your recipes for un-marinated birds on fresh game; the more exotic marinated formulas are at their best with well hung birds. Red wine marinades are in order: white wine marinades are best reserved for fresh meat.

If you have not tried well aged game prepared by red wine marin-ades in continental style you have a marvellous treat to learn to treasure.

Procede with caution. Use great care cleaning birds for the marin-ade, progress by easy stages to longer hangings. Above all, never fool yourself on the intact character of your birds. Spoiled meat is dangerous to eat, and gives game a bad name among the uninitiated. Both are to studiously avoid!

4

THE MIXED BAG

Save for driven birds and marsh fowl, all French, Spanish and Italian small game hunts produce mixed bags. Even deer hunters usually encounter birds and hares. The vast popularity of the combination guns - two or three tubes - everywhere north of the midi of France is a function of this situation where seasons, species and hunt methods overlap continuously. In central United States latitudes the same can often be true, especially in the kitchen since some small game hangs and other does not. It is not, then unusual for serious uplanders to accumulate ready-to-cook woodcock, grouse, pheasant, river bed ducks and rabbit, hare and squirrels. At least, it can often be arranged if desired. Here are a few provincial solutions to this delightful question, simple but rich in contrasts.

TROIS COGS
Choose a large well aged pheasant,a small fresh grouse and a woodcock - or several such trios. Prepare for roasting, rub all with butter well seasoned with sage, fresh pepper and fresh lemon juice. Stuff the grouse with the whole 'cock, the pheasant with the grouse. It will help to cut leg joints and wings off the grouse or possibly to "half split" it to compact it. But try at least to stuff everything, cut or attached, in the pheasant.

Roast tightly covered for a very long time in slow heat - 275 degrees - brushing with more sage butter as needed. Try to add no water, but by tight covering and basting to loose little moisture into the oven.

When thoroughly tender brown uncovered at 375 degrees briefly, and add flour to the pan liquid to make a thick gravy, thinning as need be with a tiny bit of dry sherry. A stunning but delicate "essence of fowl" is the result. Serve with mild vegetables or a simple salad and a light white or rose wine.

At the end of a glorious week of golden hills, ripe yellow fields and purpling, browning brush in the long shadows of old farm houses and stately oaks west of Paris, the last evening had come. Everyone had started out in a aged Mercedes from a belle-epoque apartment under the gaze of the Eiffel Tower, and in the morning the grand doubles, the venerable leather cases and tired but relaxed Parisians and their guests would trek back, through historic chartres, to the quieter autumn glory of the city of light, to office, lecture hall, courtroom.

A huge blaze of hardwood and sparkling sarments (knotty butts of grapevine wood) roared under the open grill in a cool, almost chilly evening in the sprawling farm house, half open on a porch where all week pheasants, duck, partridges and rabbits had hung. Towards last some woodcock had come through, as well.

Now all these were presented on a huge platter, cleaned, split and flattened for broiling, and on another assorted cut lemons, limes, tomatoes, apples, and a tureen of soft butter deeply colored by ground fresh parsley, coarse pepper and rich blood red port. Everyone had a long fork and cuts of game were personally broiled to suit each tongue liberally dipped in the ported butter. The aroma of this orgy defies description. Fresh green peppers, grand yellow onions, dipped in the pot and lightly grilled, between quarters of pheasant and duck and partridge, completed the picture. Most took tomatoes and apples raw.

If you have a comparable mixed bag of young game which needs no marinating, what can be better than to duplicate this homely wonder? Nothing in the sparkling wonder of the Tour d' Argent, amid crystal and silver and haut cuisine, overlooking the Seine and a flood lit Notre Dame, could be more memorable.

GAME STUFFED PHEASANT AND GROUSE

Stuffings made from game meat are not uncommon in northern Europe. Here is a strong one to use with a brace of old well hung pheasant cocks.

In a heavy skillet brown hickory smoked bacon or side pork to get a good bath of hot fat. Fry very lightly 2 to 2½ cups of finely diced rabbit or squirrel or venison trimmings - or even a combination of all three if for some reason you have it so - for each bird; remove from heat, add 1 cup raw onion finely chopped, sage and laurel to taste but fairly liberally; pack the birds very tightly (meat stuffings don't expand like cereals but contract!), truss or sew up, and lard the exterior with thick sliced bacon. Roast tightly covered for a long time at low temperature until very tender, open pan, remove bacon and brown before serving. Try not to add any water to pan drippings but do baste occasionally during cooking. A bit of flour and ruby port in these concentrated drippings make a sweetly rich gravy. Here it is appropriate to add good tart (that is home made!) current or red berry jelly to the gravy just before serving.

Overlapping grouse/deer seasons make venison liver an excellent grouse stuffing possibility. Dice liver, but saute in butter not bacon or pork; add diced onion as above, but much easier on the sage, no laurel, oregano and thyme, again not much. Stuff big, lightly hung ruffs, lard with butter, roast slowly, covered, use only pan juice to baste. Brown lightly as above before serving, use red burgundy rather than port in the gravy and no conserve or jelly. This is delightful but much more delicate than the squirrel/rabbit stuffed pheasant.

MEAT AND FISH: THE COOPERATIVE CHEF

There must still be many American restaurants which offer a snippet of pre-portioned steak and pre-portioned lobster, quick broiled in vegetable oil veil over gas burners, reconstituted lemon juice in margarine, and give it a drole title: Surf 'n Turf.

My prejudices show. But fish and meat, fruits of sea and lake and river by those of marsh and field are a natural combination, altogether inevitable in the south of France where the fields, the marshes and the rugged Provencal hills all yield up a bountiful harvest from August until Advent. Our Wisconsin, Michigan and Minnesota falls bring together similar grand harvest as do those of old New England, Quebec and the American northwest. The cook must follow suit when the hunters and disciples of Peter bring home rare treasure.

5

BIG GAME

BOUILLI

Bouilli is a country recipe for French beef - usually older, leaner (but also more flavorful, even gamey) than any of our own. Boiled beef does not sound imaginitive, to say the least. But skillfully seasoned and accompanied by crisp salad, dark bread and robust wine it makes a hearty Burgundian mid-morning "dejeuner" well suited to country appetites.

I propose it - or a variation with which I am familiar - as an ideal preparation for moose, elk, or older venison, even older western antelope, because it tenderizes without marinating or masking.

Cut meat into larger than usual stew sized cubes - 2" x 2" at average. Cover with water into which you have put sage, oregano, thyme, laurel, bay, sweet basil and summer savory. Bring to a boil and then simmer all day covered, like a stew or soup. (Don't salt until just before serving, if then!)

When meat is butter tender, *but not before,* add the following fresh vegetables, coarsely cut or torn up:

Yellow onions	A few heads of broccoli
Celery	Leeks (greens) if available
Green Pepper	Greens of fresh beets
Fresh garlic	Parsley

Continue cooking just until these greens are lightly cooked and still crisp, and retain their colors. Serve directly from the big pot into preheated, shallow tureens. And don't neglect a dark bread, chewey and filling, and robust Cotes du Rhone of a peasant cru - that is, full of life and energy, even a trifle coarse in its richness.

CURED BEAR MEAT FOR SALADS

Marinate thin sliced fresh bear, be sure to remove all fat. Smoke slowly over hemlock bark until very done. Cut julienne in salads, or for open sandwich hors d' oeuvres.

5-days in crockery marinade:

Cider vinegar (5%)   Fresh rind of lemon
Brown sugar to taste   Laurel bay leaves
Crushed cloves
Fennel seed
Summer Savory
Sweet Basil

SPRING BLACK BEAR

Bear is not a prime gourmet meat. Nonetheless there are some very civilized ways to prepare it if you wish. Essential is to have young fresh bear meat.

Carefully remove all fat from roastable cuts of bear, divide into slabs about 3" x 4" x 2" and simmer until 2/3 done in water to which you've added cider vinegar and lemon juice.

Fry in a heavy pan some thick chunks of hickory cured bacon and reserve; slice the boiled bear into thin cross pieces and discard the water in which it cooked. Brown the thin *tranches* lightly in the pan in bacon fat, be careful not to over cook them.

Line a casserole with *fresh raw* rhubarb cut rather coarsely, then a layer of thin sliced limes and lemons, then browned bear; repeat the layers, compressing them tightly. When firm pour bacon drippings over the whole, dot top with the bacon and finish liquid with about 2/3 cup vinegar to which you've added a few teaspoons of dark brown sugar (easy on the sugar!). Cover tightly, bake slowly (325 degrees at most) for a long, long time until rhubarb is almost a sauce.

Serve in hot tureens right out of the casserole with hot, dark bread a very astringent green salad (for example watercress with roguefort or bleu cheese dressing) and a sparkling burgundy.

If you thought bear a dish for boors, this could change your mind.

VENISON

Each winter venison makes more enemies in the kitchen and dining room. Naturally old tough deer, hard run, ill transported, inefficiently cleaned, improperly hung, frozen in tiny cuts in home freezers, are never going to be good. Venison should be hung in cold above freezing for a long period, cut up *as used,* and cooked according to age and size. In a French butcher shop, in fall, young deer hang in the hide and a roast or rack or sirloin is cut off, in the hide, as each customer asks for it. Pretend your barn or shed is such a place for December! If you have more venison than you need give a party or give it outright. Frozen venison is dry and rarely good. It needs doctoring rather than cooking and that is the tone of most venison recipes in the press - to rescue it and render it edible rather than to savor it. A pity.

Accompanying are four typically unfancy European venison procedures as the bourgeoise country or city home maker might use. Each has a different type of cut in mind and all are homely adaptions of traditional "haut cuisine" of graceful days of old when French chefs in the chateaux of all central Europe preserves were hunted out each fall and noble stags were hung in cobbled courtways by liveried game keepers, and grand wine was served on tables in sight of the vineyards where it grew. Recipes, in a word, to celebrate, not to disguise.

If you have good young venison, well kept, lovingly and knowingly treated, you will appreciate them: a wonderful change from the boorish things that happen to venison in too many thoughtless hands.

My first introduction to venison was at Cafe Bohemia on Chicago's west loop edge - served on a big bed of savory wild rice; the chops were, juicy, rosy and tender, broiled to a turn and drizzled in a spicy marinade sauce. The incentive to continue this most youthful memory, and my repugnance for "hash house" deer cookery, is perhaps understandable. (I believe that evening also marked by first experience with a superb chateau - neuf - du - pape, reigning king of venison wines . . . small wonder its vivid recall!)

VENISON LIVER ROLLS

Steam and chill (about an hour) large outside leaves of green cabbage or two. Don't steam done, just enough to make them limp, rollable.

Slice a fresh venison liver as nearly paper thin as you can the day before and marinate in rich red wine into which you've bruised a clove or so of garlic for each liver slice. To prepare:

Dredge each thin liver slice, thoroughly drained and dried off, in flour rather well seasoned with curry powder; work in thoroughly. Put a thick layer of butter on each cabbage leaf, then a matching size skewer with toothpicks or a couple of clean slivers of cedar. Bake surrounded with large mushrooms, open pan, *baste frequently,* using marinade to keep copious pan liquid. Liberal buttering of leaves is better than adding any as you progress. Hold the oven rather smartly at 400 degrees, rolls are done when very tender to the puncture of another toothpick.

Variation: Two cabbage leaves per roll (outside the first leaf) thick sliced bacon inside next to liver in place of butter; broil over a slow maple fire until done as above. Substitute another vegetable for the mushrooms, brush with oil to keep exterior cabbage from drying and burning. Keep the fire slow, please!

VENISON IN CABBAGE

Buy the biggest freshest cabbages you can find, red or green. Cut top off 1/3 of the way down, keep the "hat" intact. Hollow out the bottom to leave a big, hollow, but firm, shell.

Saute' in a heavy skillet chipped hickory smoked bacon, side pork or even smoked ham enough to make a good layer of fat; add and saute' diced venison trimmings from loin, or if you are feeling flush, diced tenderloin of venison, plus diced onion. Red pepper, sweet basil, summer savory, a *bit* of white pepper, and liberal sloshes of cider vinegar, a whiff of brown sugar (very optional!)

Spoon saute'd mixture into cabbage, replace top, pin with toothpicks and bake slowly, well supported, in a buttered casserole. When cabbage is very tender transport gently to table after heating a bit hotter than baking temperature and open and serve, about 1 cabbage to 2 persons. Dark beer is perfect here!

You may have liquid left over in the skillet; put the cuttings from the cabbage interior in these drippings, cook in the oven and reserve to reheat as a delicious side dish the following day or as a cold salad component.

SMOKED SUGAR PRESERVED VENISON

It is probably a sin to grind venison trimmings into plebian American "burgers" or sausage. To repent, try this northern European approach. The result should be a savorous substitute for smoked old fashioned beef or ham in any application where no fat content is necessary - for mince meat fillings, to flavor salads, pate fillings, stuffings for poultry and game, and countless other gourmet employments.

Trim all fat from cuttings and dice, don't grind, keeping pieces as large as possible. The best size and shape is a rectangle or square about a scant 1/8" thick, similar to thick sliced bacon, with an inch or so on each side. Salt and pepper lightly if at all and soak 4 - 5 days covered with cider vinegar in a glass or crockery vessel, with pickling spice mix a combination of dill, clove, fenugreek, fennel and laurel among others, best bought preportioned in the store.

Drain the meat, reserve marinade; smoke with green maple on a fine gauge rack until *very well done.* If you have access to hickory, add it to the fire in the form of damp chips. (Naturally these bits will finish faster than larger pieces of meat.)

Add brown sugar to the marinade rather liberally - 1/4 to 1/3 cup sugar to 1 cup liquid, then lace with a good plain brandy or half and half brandy and dark Puerto Rican rum. Replace meat in liquid, put the whole to simmer on the range in a pot until thoroughly hot, bottle in glass, seal tightly and hold in the refrigerator. This smoked/pickled meat will keep a long time and can be used at will for the applications noted. The only additional preparation needed may be finer chopping for fillings or tarts of various sour/sweet sour flavor. (If you cut the meat finer, add raisins, lemon peel and twice the sugar plus a bit of cornstarch to thicken during the heating, you will have magnificent ready to use mincemeat of different and incomparable flavor!)

VENISON CHOPPED LOUIS

(This preparation is an adaption of the famous "agneau a la martyr", favorite luxury of the gouty, and overfed brother of Louis XVI, who after his brother's (timely) beheading, enjoyed a sumptuous exile as well as a short period of kingship, equally sumptuous and ineffective in other realms.)

Use young, tender loin chops, of a yearling deer, well fattened on Wisconsin corn belt country.

Cut the chops quite thickly - over ½ inch to ¾ inch. Marinate overnight in a gentle red wine, only a touch of crushed garlic, if that. Meanwhile take good fat loin pork chops, bone them but leave as much fat as possible. Cut these very thin, or ask your butcher to do so - about a scant ¼ inch or less. Surround each venison chop with the thin "blankets" of pork, with thin slices of white onion separating pork and venison, and pin together as much as possible without puncturing the lean meat of the venison. Put these "sandwiches" on a rather hot maple grill and turn very frequently so the venison is bathed in the juices generated about it by pork and onion. Broil until the pork is overdone, virtually burned black. At no time should the venison see the fire in person.

Serve the chops, after removing their coat, on a hot platter bedded in their onion slices. They should be incredibly moist, done to medium rosy, and delicate. Garnish with chopped parsley and dabs of fresh butter and lemon slices.

A light red wine and a crisp green vegetable is indicated - this is an exquisitely fresh rather than a "hearty" way to prepare young venison.

SAUTEED VENISON LIVER (FOIE DE DAIM MOUTARDE)

A lot of venison liver is fresh fried over campfires - and this is a reward for the day's work not to be downed if done nicely. But liver of young venison is a gourmet treat - better than that of calf or pork by far. If you are close to home here is a fabulously simple Italian recipe.

Wash and dry deer liver, remove any waste, and slice into very thin slices just big enough in area to handle with your best and biggest spatula. Soak the slices overnight in a shallow tray of red burgundy, no spices really necessary.

Put a lot of butter - a pound or so - in your iron skillet, and slowly saute there coarsely chopped mild onion or shallots, and big chunks of fresh mushrooms. Accumulate these in a hot oven proof dish or deep platter and hold hot in the oven at about 275 degrees or less. Leave butter in pan.

Dry the marinated liver slices and dredge them evenly in fine quality dry mustard. Each should be as dry and smooth as if "floured" for frying. Bring your butter to saute temperature and lace with *fresh* lemon juice squeezed over the pan. Saute the liver slices quickly, don't get them over done and put *only one* or *two* in the pan at a time. They should be golden but short of brown - just past rare, *towards medium.* Accumulate in the oven on top of your platter of onion and mushroom.

When all the liver is done add the marinade wine to the butter in the skillet, season to taste but delicately - a trifle of *tarragon* is the crucial spice here. Pour this over your hot platter and serve piping.

Again, a delicate rather than a hearty preparation, with which a light red or even - heresy! - a rose of character is delightful. Best choice of all is the very light Italian Lambrusco now widely and inexpensively available. (Always choose the "young" Lambruscos - 7 to 9% alcohol - for lighter meals.)

VENISON DRESDEN

Here is a superb "saurbrauten" type preparation for poorer venisons: lunker bucks, older or hard run deer, and far north woods foragers in general.

Cut raw aged meat in generous cubes 1 to 1½ inches square. Soak in a crock with a heavy red wine vinegar and cut garlic and white onions for as long as practical up to 5 days - more might not hurt. Cover the meat liberally, *don't* use cider vinegar!

Saute the onions and garlic slowly in a big iron skillet or pot with chunks of good hickory smoked bacon coarsely cut. Pat your meat chunks dry and pound seasoned flour into each very liberally, then brown gently in the bacon/onion combination on the stove. When crisply browned, cover scantily with red wine, add bay leaves and into a medium oven tightly covered.

Meanwhile use the reserved vinegar marinade to moisten a casserole dish of finely chopped red and green cabbage. The raw cabbage should be at least half covered with vinegar, add more if you are short. Into the oven with this casserole.

Bake both slowly half the day, peek occasionally to keep pots moist and well turned in their liquids. (The cabbage will cook well done faster than the meat; it can come out for a time if necessary.) Some add a whif of sugar to the cabbage. Not I!

When meat chunks are really tender, mix the two pots together and add thick sour cream to which you have added enough good grade dry mustard to color it yellow. Put the uncovered "ragout" back in the oven to "get used" to the new proximity of meat and cabbage, and to dry up a bit if it is wet. Serve very hot, sprinkled with a bit of paprika for appearance.

A big strong burgundy is demanded, and a fresh hot rye bread with lots of good butter is a perfect foil for this typically German interpretation of the royal game.

VENISON SIRLOIN ROLL (FILET DE CHEVREUIL EPINARDS)

Have on hand: boned out whole tenderloin from a young deer; include sirloin if you need more meat - or use two tenderloins; 1 lb. fresh spinach; 2-3 lb. slab of hickory smoked bacon, the real thing.

Cut the tenderloin lengthwise just enough to start a "flap" of meat, then "peel" it with even lengthwise strokes until you have a large, flat filet about ½" thick which can be rolled up or spread out. Marinate your flattened tenderloin in red wine for at least a day.

Cut half the spinach into coarse bits; cut 1/3 of the bacon into coarse chunks ¼" x ¼" and soak for an hour or so in wine vinegar the day of preparation. Spread the marinated, flattened tenderloin with cut spinach and bacon chunks, roll tightly up; coat the outside of the "rolled" tenderloin with washed leaves of spinach, then with the balance of the bacon cut into thick strips. Truss the roll tightly with butcher's twine - don't skewer or puncture the meat.

Roast the whole in a tight pan, keeping moist with a bit of water added to drippings but just enough to prevent burning on. A rack in the pan is helpful: use a mild 275 - 300 degree oven for a 3 - 4 hours of slow cooking. During last half hour when meat is tender (try an *end* with table fork, don't puncture center of roll!) open the pan, turn oven up to brown exterior bacon at about 375 degrees. Add marinade wine, and vinegar used for bacon chunks, to pan drippings, and reduce in a skillet adding a touch of sage, oregano and cayenne pepper - not much of any. (Bacon has already provided salt!)

Serve the rolled tenderloin on a hot platter, slice in thick 1½" segments to serve. Keep the drippings sauce hot at table in a chafing dish and drench each slice of tenderloin as you put it on a guest's plate.

Both sirloin and sauce can be reheated gracefully the second day but there will seldom be leftovers. A burgundy is indicated and a rich augratin potato, dry and cheesy, is a good accompaniment.

6

FRESHWATER FISH

"It is scarcely surprising that most Americans with cultivated tastes don't appreciate your grand fresh water game fish," a European friend said to me this fall. "You murder them in the kitchen, or before they even get to the kitchen.

I see his point. The grease soaked, old, frozen fish served Friday night hash house style with pre-breaded french fries and grocery store tartar sauce in countless homes and restaurants scarcely tend to make one an enthusiast.

My critical friend is a gourmet who has traveled the world and who is no mean cook. We spent an evening discussing his ways with our game fish - ways which are a revelation and a delight - and make dining with this gentleman an experience. Here are his comments and recipes:

"Fish are delicate, and ought to be prepared fresh. Frozen fish is always a sad approximation. But if you must freeze fresh game fish, always do so in a waxed carton in a solid block of ice, and always lace the water with fresh lemon juice."

"Better yet, catch just enough for each day's meal, rush them onto ice and clean the fish thoroughly just as rapidly as possible after catching."

WALLEYE

"Frying destroys both texture and flavor. Concentrate on other preparations which enhance the fragile flavor and lovely texture of really fresh game fish. If you must "fry", do so vienna style; with your 'walleyed' pike fillet this is an excellent dish and the fish is robust enough to react well."

"Use fresh fillets, and rub each with a fresh cut lemon squeezing juice liberally. Coat each fillet with very lightly salted or unsalted flour, carefully packing flour into the surface of the flesh - no brown bag shaking, please! Then coat each fillet - again gently and thoroughly - with a lightly beaten egg white with two yolks and enough cream to make an egg nog thick batter. Then dredge each fillet in yellow corn meal until a thick yellow coating envelops each fillet. Keep these very cold - ice box or even freezer cold for a short period - while you bring a generous layer of butter to moderately high temperature in a heavy skillet. Saute the fillets slowly and carefully one at a time until uniformly crisp. Handle the fragile fillets with a pair of spatulas to avoid breaking or crumbling of the coating.

As each fillet is well browned and solid on its exterior, transfer it to a rack in an open oven pan and allow to finish cooking slowly until very tender inside the crust. Each fillet should be dry and free of fresh grease or of soggy spots. Meanwhile, as the fillets finish in the oven, strain your pan drippings, add more butter, a little finely chopped shallot or green-top onion, never a harsh onion and about ¼ of its volume in fresh squeezed lemon juice. Mix thoroughly and into the oven, to hold. Serve each fillet on a dry leaf of deep green lettuce, garnished at the side with lemon slices and lime slices and keep the lemon butter piping hot in a chafing dish on the table. This simple preparation makes walleye a real experience even for a fussy connoisseur."

MUSKIE

"Your muskellunge is often actually ignored as a table delicacy even by those who like to hunt him - a pity, for he is a rare treat, superior in savor to many of the large fish so vaunted in European cookery. Here is a regal preparation worthy of the king:"

"Clean the fish as rapidly as possibly can be done, keep it very cold. Cut into very large steaks, clear across the whole fish keeping to one inch - not less - of thickness. The result will resemble a large salmon or swordfish steak. On a large musky the biggest steaks can be split in two at the center. For this purpose the center third - or perhaps better, the forward half of a big fish is prime. Save the rear third or so for other uses.

"Soak each steak for a day, *inside a very cold ice box, please,* covered by a mix of ¾ white dry wine, ¼ fresh lemon juice, and some finely sliced big onions and crushed garlic cloves.

"Prepare a bed of maple coals in an open broiler, plan on a long fire, not overly hot. Hickory added to the wood is a bonus. Broil each steak carefully, turning gently with two large spatulas brushing continuously with butter. The steaks should be very crisply browned with a thick but never even slightly burned exterior which holds each slab of fish whole and in form. Transfer to a shallow oven pan, cover with marinade, a bit more butter, and bake slowly until the drippings are reduced and steaks are extremely tender inside their crusty exterior. (Test with a very fine fork or toothpick.)"

"Make a platter of finely chopped walnut meats and chopped cooked mushrooms, tossing thoroughly with butter, and hold this very hot until serving. Place steaks when done on this bedding, partly enveloping them in it. Pour oven pan sauce over the whole, garnish with fresh parsley, paprika and a few slices of lemon, lime, fresh radishes for color."

FISH STOCK

"Every fish cook needs stock - much reduced fish bouillon. The small mid-summer northerns no one likes, carefully cleaned but with all the edges, as well as bones and cuttings from filleting and preparing other fish are put in a very big pot and simmered for several days. When reduced to a thick rich fish broth strain out all solid matter pressing out all broth. Discard this and add cut up fresh tomatoes with peelings, a few sliced onions, bay leaf and fennel to the stock, reduce again until very concentrated. This can be kept hot on the range, for a short period in the ice box (in glass, please) and for longer in the home freezer. Always heat to boiling before using stock that has cooled!"

"There are three main uses for this stock:

1. As a medium to poach whole smaller panfish or fillets of larger fish. Always poach very slowly and gently over a low fire. Add a trifle of lemon juice to the pan; when the poached fish are flaky remove, drain and hold hot. Reduce the pan fluid, thicken just a bit with flour, generous butter, seasoning to taste, serve hot over hot poached fish on the hot platter. (Recommended for making a delicacy of blue gills and sunfish, this is an ideal procedure for the popular little perch which is an abundant winter harvest as well and is often at its very best in cold months.)

2. As base for a sauce to put over any other sauceable presentation, such as baked or the vienna style suggested for walleyed pike.

Reduce the stock slightly, thicken with egg yolks and heavy cream over very gentle heat, butter very liberally, and add white dry table wine just moments before serving over fish on a hot platter, so the wine does not cook appreciably. Variations of spices are added at the last minutes of making such a sauce: over a baked fish tarragon is especially savorous.

3. As a soup. Heat ½ as much stock as you need soup; add a bit of tarragon, oregano, sage and even a bit more finely minced mild onion when stock boils, often bits of fresh fish which you are very certain are free of bones! When any freshly added fish is cooked, add milk slowly until you have a bit more than ¾ the desired quantity; finish out with heavy cream and white wine. preferably chablis, always chalk dry. (When adding milk and cream have the stock mix just warm, not hot; likewise make sure milk and cream are out in the range area long enough to lose their ice box chill. Sharp contrasts of temperature create curdling and mixing woes.) Soup should now be heated up to piping hot, spooned into preheated bowls, a big square of fresh butter floated in the center, and then, paprika to enhance the slightly rosy tint from the tomato in the stock. Fresh diced parsley is a perfect garnish."

TROUT

My friend thinks that all our trout - including splake and coho salmon - should be prepared very simply, broiled in the open air, slowly, over maple, well basted with lemon butter during broiling. Complex sauces or preparations spoil these delicate creations miserably.

These simple and elegant procedures prove that our superb gamefish are equal or superior to anything regularly served in Europe or the grand establishments of cuisine stateside. Well prepared, fresh Wisconsin delicacies are far superior in my belief, to ninety percent of the less than fresh but prestigious "seafood" so dear to well heeled restaurant hounds in the metropolitan hub bub.

If brook and rainbow trout are too precious, sacred and delicate for any but the simplest most elegant preparations, the northern Wisconsin Lake Trout is perhaps sufficiently ordinary to tempt a "fancy" recipe, or even a homely recipe. Here are two in each catagory.

TROUT LENINGRAD

Saute whole cleaned lake trout slowly in butter with liberal coarse ground white and black peppercorns until almost done in a heavy oven-proof pan. Cover with dry French Vermouth, add a few lemon wedges, slashed and squeezed into the wine. Bake until fish is totally flaky and liquid reduced, holding oven at about 350 degrees. Just before serving, heat a beaker of Smirnoff Vodka in the oven along with the fish, pour over and flame just as you present it to your guests. Serve with a heavy cream-sauced vegetable, or perhaps potatoes au gratin.

TROUT AUX FEUILLES

Split cleaned lake trout in two along the spine, rub each halved fish with fresh lemon, then dust with sage. Wrap each half in a liberal leaf - two if needbe - of the crispest romain lettuce you can muster, and lay snugly in an oven casserole dish well wiped with olive oil. On top of the well wrapped trout spread a layer of coarsely torn parsley, spinach, and finely chopped white onion, a bit of coarse pepper, and liberal dabs of butter throughout. Cover tightly and bake until well done (drive a straw or toothpick down into bottom layer gently to test fish) and then open casserole, swim with heavy cream, sprinkle top with grated romano cheese and paprika and allow a bit longer for the whole to "go through the layers" before serving. Use wooden or blunt silver spoons to retrieve the wrapped trout at the table, arrange on pre-warmed plates, creamy sauce spooned over, lemon wedges on the side. A rose wine - or white - is quite appropriate. Elegant and trouble free.

BREAKFAST TROUT

There is nothing European about this presentation but it is common enough in approach for lake fish in northern countries in spite of a certain homeliness.

Dip cut trout in a butter of a touch of flour, egg yolks and heavy cream, seasoned with finely rubbed sweet basil; then into coarse yellow corn meal, then into a heavy skillet of hot butter into which you have sliced fresh cloves of garlic. When cuts are crisply done remove to an oven rack to dry out (about 275 degrees) while you add a bit of cream to the pan to make a sauce to pour over crisp trout at the table.

BARBEQUED TROUT

Peel a pile of fresh sweet corn and reserve the "shucks" in a bowl of lemon laced water. In a skillet over part of your barbeque fire fry up small cubes of salt pork to make a good bath of fat. Cut raw corn off ears and fry it very slowly, covered, in this fat. Wrap cleaned trout, rubbed with butter in wet corn shucks very thickly, and pin if necessary. Cook over medium coals until corn shucks are virtually carbonised. Keep your fire on the low side so you can cook slowly and make fish and corn come out done at the same time. To serve, pour fat off the well done corn, season with a touch of tarragon, and use it to smother your freshly unwrapped trout. But again, drain excess so you have flavor without greasiness.

Fresh baking powder biscuits go superbly with either of the last two preparations.

WALLEYED PIKE PROVENCALE

Clean and cut into large serving pieces enough walleye to loosely fill a deep casserole dish. Arrange with quartered fresh tomatoes, coarsely cut celery, white onion, bruised fresh garlic, torn up parsley, and sprinkle with fennel, sweet basil, sage (optional) and a very few crushed dill seeds. Drench thoroughly with olive oil, cover tightly, bake slowly for a long period. Serve directly into shallow pre-heated tureens, with a mild green salad (try our watercress and roguefort cheese suggestion!) and a chalky dry white burgundy.

MUSKELLUNGE NAPOLI

Use a conventional Italian pasta sauce recipe - ours is simply pureed tomatoes, green peppers, onion, garlic, oregano, tarragon, a trifle of red wine and a still smaller trifle of red wine vinegar, and some fine cut mozzarella cheese.

Into a mature casserole of this sauce, simmering, put fine to medium cubed boned muskellunge meat and simmer until fish is done but not disintegrated. You should have much fish and not too much sauce.

Serve over hot, steaming piles of long spaghetti or other hot Italian pasta, and top with grated romano or parmesan cheese. Here a light or medium red wine is indicated.

Maybe more little perch are caught in a northern summer than all other species put together. One can make a bit of festivity even over perch! Sophisticates may simmer them for fish stock, but here are two different preparations for decent size fresh perch, which often are extremely abundant. We assume you are sick of or disgusted by greasy little breaded limplings soaked in commercial frying oil.

PERCHE A LA BROCHE

Carefully wash some fresh lemons and cut small yellow onions into firm wedges. Clean some decent sized perch and prepare a hot maple and hickory fire (hemlock bark is a good hickory substitute). Slice a couple of big Idaho potatoes in thin, 1/8" slices.

Squeeze lemons into a bowl of virgin olive oil, season with thyme, bay, oregano and bruised fresh garlic. Dip potato slices in lemon-oil mix while you stuff each perch with a wedge of onion and a tid bit of cut lemon rind. Skewer through lemon and onion, gently, so all hangs firmly together. Separate fish with a slice of oil soaked potato. Broil, brushing constantly with oil mixture until fish flake and potato slices are crisp and puffy. Hold over a cooler part of the fire (or in the oven at 275 degrees) until you have a brochet of six or so fish ready for each guest. Serve from a hot platter, drizzled with remains of oil-lemon mix.

PATE STUFFED PERCH

Dice fine some boneless panfish meat and saute in butter with chives; add toasted bread crumbs and an egg yolk, thyme and sage to taste, and stuff fresh perch with the mixture. Wrap each perch in a spinach leaf and perhaps pin to keep together. Bake until done in a shallow pan in the juices to which fresh butter is periodically added as a basting medium. Baste continually and when perch is very done, serve directly "en casserole", with little dippers and beakers of sauce made by diluting pan drippings with fresh lemon juice, a trace of tabasco, and dry vermouth after all heating of the sauce is complete. Metal (silver or stainless) sauce beakers can be gently pre-warmed and will keep the sauce warm for each diner.

ENGLISH PERCH

Fry little perch - your littlest - gently in butter with slivered or sliced almonds, chives, fresh mushrooms and a whiff of good Worcestershire sauce. When flaky done remove fish and keep warm in a slow oven on a rack. Into the skillet with mushrooms and almonds pour a rich Yorkshire pudding batter (ours is egg yolk, flour, heavy cream, baking powder if desired, smartly beaten together). When your "pudding" is set and done cut in liberal squares and serve on a hot platter with perch and parsley garnish. Surprising! An elegant light luncheon with green salad and chablis.

REGAL MUSKELLUNGE SALAD

Hickory smoke large cubes of left-over muskellunge meat - probably tail ends or trimmings from baked or broiled dishes. These should be very thoroughly smoked and held cold, drizzled with lemon and lime fresh squeezed.

Heat to simmer a cup of white wine vinegar for each two guests to serve; add per cup a pinch of cardamon and a half teaspoon premium dry mustard.

Tear up fresh spinach, red leaf lettuce and watercress in an amount equal to 1½ the volume of your cubed smoked fish. Slice hard cooked eggs for topping. Before serving toss greens and fish together; garnish in a large warm bowl with eggs.

Add cognac to hot vinegar about 1/3 cup to the cup, remove from heat, spin in 1/3 cup fine salad oil and a touch of soft butter, and drizzle hot dressing over salad. Allow to wilt and rest on the table during hors d' oeuvre hour. Serve in individual room temperature bowls, being careful to scoop dressing liberally from bottom of serving bowl over individual portions.

LAKE SUPERIOR WHITEFISH LIVERS

This rich liver delicacy may be prepared in any way appropriate to game bird liver, or simply sauteed in butter or even bacon drippings. Three particularly special recipes follow, including a piquant hors d' oeuvre; each requires very fresh livers. Best is to meet the fishing boats like the Chequamegon Bay gulls!

EN PATE

Make and roll thin a rich, short pate crust, with an egg yolk added for color; divide into squares 6" on a side. Sautee whitefish livers in fresh butter and sliced garlic cloves. When nearly done arrange livers on squares of crust, add raw diced white onion, oregano, thyme to taste. Fold each square into a triangle, wet edges and seal tightly. Bake in a hot oven until golden flaky, brush with egg yolk lightly beaten for a crusty final appearance. Serve piping hot with deep green crisp salad for light lunch, with California Chablis.

A LA MAYONNAISE

Poach white fish livers in good dry Chablis, gently, let liquid reduce itself to very little. Drain and chill livers. Mix cooled poaching wine with mayonnaise, dry mustard and cognac to make a creamy yellow sauce. For each cocktail hors d' oeuvre line a chilled silver bowl with a leaf of lettuce and a slice of raw yellow onion; cold livers on top of this, followed by a total covering of the sauce, garnish with paprika and a curl of lime rind. This can replace shrimp cocktail before a regal repast. Be sure all components and dishes are icy cold. (Try prechilling silver or glass servers in the freezer for 30 - 40 minutes).

FOIE AU FROMAGE

Bake a good 5 pounds of Idaho potatoes fluffy and done; remove potato from skins. Cut skins in strips and crisp in deep butter with green onions and peppers.

Mix potato pulp with enough romano and parmesan cheese, finely grated, to color it rich yellow, adding egg yolk to link the mix. Don't use milk or cream here.

Make a thick layer of potato cheese mix in a well buttered casserole and into the oven at about 300 degrees. See that the mixture climbs the buttered walls of the casserole and makes a "tub" in the center.

Saute white fish livers done in butter - onion, after removing potato skins; drain and arrange in the "tub" of the casserole in a thick layer. Crisp potato skins on top of this, followed by a good rich layer of grated cheese of a light dry sort - more romano or dry provolone is excellent. Up oven to 400 degrees until cheese is melted, garnish with snipped up pimento or wild red peppers. Serve hot out of the casserole with broad spoons to preserve the layers as much as you can.

BOILED NORTHERN PIKE

Cut fresh cold northerns in serving chunks. Bring to a boil a kettle of lightly salted water to which you have added liberal bruised fresh garlic, cloves, bay leaves, fennel and sweet basil.

Put pike cold in boiling kettle; it should rise to the surface as cooking is completed. Drain and serve on a hot platter with new steamed potatoes - plum sized - the whole liberally drenched with parsley chive butter.

PANFISH WITH ONION SAUCE

Put fine whole yellow onions and a few cubes of salt pork in a kettle of water - no salt needed - and bring to a boil. When onions begin to be close to done add fresh cold whole panfish - perch, blue-gills, sunfish, small crappies. These will float to surface when done, at which point remove them and keep hot, drained of liquid. Retrieve onions, drain, reduce to a puree in a blender. Thicken this puree gently with a bit of flour, butter and fresh heavy cream, and pour over fish on a hot serving platter.

BROILED LAKE SUPERIOR WHITEFISH NANTES

This preparation is arbitrarily named after a particular sentimental reminiscence but it is typical of a northern French chateau preparation - bourgeoise style.

Choose very large, very fresh whitefish, leave heads and tails on and split ventral side far back. Stuff with torn hand fulls of watercress and cubes of lime, flesh and skin, carefully pre-washed of course. Lard sides of fish with thick slices of hickory smoked bacon or side pork, and truss with butchers twine if necessary to hold together - pinning with picks of wood may not be enough.

Broil high over a smart maple fire until bacon is charred, fish almost flaky. Finish slowly in the oven and serve with Dijon sauce:

Reduce an already dense fish bouillon to half (see our suggestions elsewhere for fish stock from cuttings), thicken with a bit of flour, over low heat, add butter to make a gilded creamy sauce, a few teaspoons of French Dijon mustard to a pint of sauce and a whisper of old Cognac.

Serve on hot individual serving plates over whitefish fresh from the oven. Robust enough for an evening dinner with a nice rose or even sparkling burgundy.

BAKED STUFFED SUPERIOR WHITEFISH

Reserve whole your largest most imposing whitefish opened wide to stuff.

Stuffing: 1/4 sauteed whitefish livers, diced; saute in butter, oregano, thyme, garlic; 1/4 diced dry French bread, 1/4 cut mushrooms (raw) 1/4 quartered walnuts.

Butter interior of each fish, stuff solidly, and cover exterior of fish with soft blended butter to make a thick coat on the cold exterior. Wrap each stuffed fish in Romaine lettuce using large leaves, as many as necessary. Truss lightly to hold together, place in a buttered oven casserole with pearl onions and tiny new potatoes, also well buttered after washing. (Unpeeled potatoes take a prettier appearance and have much more flavor).

Bake at about 325 degrees, tightly covered. Cut twine off fish to serve but leave lettuce leaves, unwrap on each warm dinner plate and arrange onions and potatoes around the periphery. Spoon juices and butter atop.

White dry wine and crisp salad is indicated; the result is rather special.

BAVARIAN PIKE BOIL

Northern Pike are reputed to be soft and fishy in high summer. Maybe. Here is a different solution to the "problem" a preparation typical of germanic cooks for large rather non delicate river and lake species.

In one saucepan cook fine shredded green cabbage and sliced carrots in cider vinegar with bay leaves. Let these simmer very done.

In a saucepan bring to boil enough light beer to boil gently all the pike you have. Cut pike in chunks, add fennel and basil and a bruised garlic clove or two to boiling beer, then pike. Cook until done at a gentle boil - not too harsh.

Reduce liquid in cabbage - carrot mix, arrange on a hot platter as a bed for drained pike; top liberally with daubs of butter at the table, paprika and parsley for garnish. Guaranteed to gild the fish adequately!

Many like dark beer or English stout with such dishes.

AUBERGINES AVEC POISSON

Cube boned fresh fish meat into ½" squares, using bass, walleye, crappie or even muskellunge. Saute lightly in butter, parsley(chopped) and chives. Drain sauteed fish and stuff into hollowed eggplant shells. Bake in a moderate oven until eggplant shells are tender.

Reserve drippings in saute pan, add heavy cream to thicken and one egg yolk if desired. Pour this creamy sauce into eggplants over fish during last moments of cooking in the oven, top with butter soaked bread crumbs and finish smartly at 375 degrees before serving on a hot platter.

Try this with a spicy astringent fruit salad for summer lunches, together with a sparkling Asti wine.

Bluegills are, after perch, the most caught and the least appreciated of northern gamefish. When large, fresh, and irridescently fresh blue, these exquisite fish deserve the elegant presentations we have suggested elsewhere - poached in wine, sauteed with butter, in various cream and fish sauces and all the rest. Here are two "regales" to add to the too tarnished little crown of our lovely little summer queen, specially appropriate for cold buffets.

A L'ITALIENNE

Heat short of smoking a skillet of olive oil; add, in this order, broken heads of cauliflower, fresh raw sweet peas, fine cut celery, thick sliced raw garlic, sweet basil, a bit of dill and fennel. When peas are crisply, lightly done, remove, drain dry, and chill in refrigerator.

Saute in the remaining well flavored olive oil the freshest of bluegills, clean, dry and whole. When fish are done, remove, chill and reserve a little of the olive oil. Mix this remaining oil into whole egg mayonnaise to make a slightly thin oily sauce.

On a chilled silver platter, lettuce leaves, chilled sauteed vegetables, quartered fresh tomatoes, chilled fish on top of this, rings of red onion to top the fish, drizzle all with your mayonnaise/oil dressing. Garnish with wedges of lemon and lime, sprigs of parsley and watercress, in the center of a gala buffet. Good enough for a champagne luncheon.

A LOEUF

Pouch fresh bluegills - the smaller ones of your catch - in white chablis of the driest tone, as directed here elsewhere. Dice hard boiled eggs sufficient to stuff the cavities of cooked fish after they are chilled thoroughly and mix in a bit of fine diced black olives. (Chill egg/olive to stuff!)

Make a sauce of remaining chablis from poaching, thickened with a bit of flour, fresh heavy cream, butter, a whiff of dry mustard and just enough dry sherry to make a rich pourable sauce. Have sauce cooled to room temperature but not chilled. Present stuffed fish on a bed of lettuce with sauce dripped over.

Variation: As above, but stuff fish with fresh watercress after chilling, mix diced eggs/olives into the sauce and present separately for each guest to put together at his will.

We presume in all these preparations that guests know these fish

62

have bones! If you are in doubt, always warn the uninitiates! (There are plenty of gorgeous preparations for boned fish for neophytes - choose intelligently.)

FILET OF WALLEYED PIKE

Boneless filet of pike can be used in any of a hundred boned fish meat preparations, of course. But the popularity of long boneless filets is legendary. Here is a simple typically northern French presentation which is more happy than greasy fried (often breaded and frozen!) restaurant or weekend summer cabin walleye.

Poach filets delicately in whole milk, adding ample fresh butter towards the end of the poaching. Do not move them about more than necessary.

Prepare a bed of fine fluffy rice in a hot buttered casserole and keep hot. When filets are done, arrange on rice, holding hot in a mild oven. In milk/butter add enough flour to slightly thicken, follow with an egg yolk per cup of liquid. Season with crushed and whisked through the sauce, enough dry sherry to give a delightfully winey aroma. Pour over fish on rice bed, serve hot with minted buttered peas cooked from fresh raw.

Good with this presentation is a rose or sparkling burgundy as well as the more traditionally correct dry white or muscadet.

MUSKELLUNGE VOYAGEURS

(This preparation is equally good for large, whole, stuffable walleyes, trout or salmon.)

Carefully clean medium sized muskellunge and cut off tail portion which does not roast up as well, leaving a large stuffable fish cut into a "V" along the ventral side (belly).

Bake some simple corn meal bread, omit sugar from your recipe (ours is simply corn meal, milk, baking powder and egg) and add rubbed sage, laurel, bay, savory, sweet basil, oregano and thyme to make a spicy fragrant batter. Make a dry bread, easy on liquid. When done crumble in a shallow pan and dry the crumbs desert crackle dry in a slow oven. Make stuffing by adding chopped celery, onions and parsley and link with as many eggs as necessary to make a workable dressing.

Butter and pepper interior of fish, stuff tightly and truss up with butcher's twine, cover with cook's cheese cloth to hold basting juice.

Bake over, not in, a pan, on a grill or rack. You will need a lot of good fresh butter - about 1½ pounds for a really big fish! Don't cheat. Bake *a long time* at about 275 degrees basting continually, keep the cheese cloth soaking and butter drizzling over and through the fish throughout cooking. About ½ hour before dinner remove cheese cloth, squeeze out butter over fish, turn oven to 350 degrees to gild the surfaces, but continue basting!

Serve on a hot platter, cut grand thick cross sections of fish and stuffing for each serving. Strain pan drippings and serve as sauce, cutting with a dribble of dry Vermouth if desired. Supply fresh cut wedges of lemon and lime to each guest.

Baked potatoes with sour cream and a light green salad are good accompaniments. If you want a different drink this combination is nicely accented by cold ale or stout!

CURRY AND SAFFRON BASS

Cut raw bass or sunfish fresh caught into serving cubes ½" x ½" with a very sharp knife. Poach gently in double boiler in *just enough* water to cover; season water with basil, bay, rosemary and just the lightest whiff of curry powder - one of the really good brands without sugar or salt in the formula.

Make a casserole dish of dry, fluffy rice with sufficient saffron in the water to make a golden color. Keep hot.

When fish is tender and seasoned water almost reduced to zero, add a trifle of fine white pepper, slowly add warm heavy cream to make a thick sauce and perhaps a teaspoon of old cognac per cup of creamed bass. Increase curry now, only if tasting the sauce encourages it.

Just prior to serving make a bed of hot rice in individual hot serving plates or tureens, put a huge dollop of fresh butter right in the middle; spoon creamed bass onto this bedding, follow with chopped fresh parsley, wedges of lemon along the side. The result is delicate but exquisite. Choose a very light chalky chablis and a mild contrasting vegetable very simply prepared.

SUMMER FISH SALAD "EN MOULES"

This elegant piece de resistance is perfect for a lunch served overlooking the lake, perhaps on the deck, with frosty cocktails of dry Vermouth garnished with curls of lemon and a fruity, cheesy dessert platter in the center of the table.

Line individual serving bowls - silver or stainless steel is superb - with washed dark leaf lettuce and pre-chill in a very cold icebox.

Salad components:
- Cubed bass and/or walleyed pike, lightly poached in white wine, not too done, firmly pre-chilled; be sure to keep your cubes boneless and fairly sizeable. As much fish as all other material together.
- Cherry tomatoes, halved
- Watercress finely torn up
- Green peppers, cubed
- Curly endive, finely torn up
- Pimientos for color or red sweet fresh peppers if your market has them.

Toss all components together in a chilly dish, dust lightly with savory, sweet basil and a touch of sage. Pile thoroughly tossed salad tightly in each prepared bowl, leave in the ice box.

Dressing:

At room temperature, equal parts of high quality whole egg mayonnaise; sour cream; cream cheese; link with enough tarragon flavored white wine vinegar to make a very thick creamy dressing.

Pour over each salad very liberally and leave in ice box. Fifteen minutes before serving, and after salads have "rested" in their dressing *at least* an hour, garnish with wedges of limes, chopped parsley and a dash of paprika.

CLAMS

Millions of raccoons cannot be wrong; the delicate, irridescently blue fresh water clams that proliferate in the sandy shallows of spring fed northern lakes can be a delicacy.

Once gathered, they are cleaned and washed just as a New England or Normandy clam. Fall may be the best time to harvest these "coguillages."

Washed, cleaned clams should be soaked in pure *fresh* lemon juice for perhaps several hours. Here are two gorgeously simple presentations very "littoral French."

Cold: Saute clams in pure chablis, gently laced with butter - almost a cross between poaching and saute process. Pour off liquid, reserve chill cooked clams smartly. Chill pan drippings, add enough pure egg mayonnaise to make a thick, creamy sauce; add a tear or two of fresh lemon juice, and a wisp of horseradish, dried and ground variety, just enough dry mustard to gild the color. (Never use prepared horseradish sauce or salad mustard in such applications!)

Present 4 to 6 clams on a bed of watercress torn up in a cold silver or glass salad plate, top with sauce liberally, garnish with a lemon wedge. A perfect appetizer or hors d' oeuvre with a crisp rye bread and (if you are rich and lucky, drink fresh young greenish Muscadet with these fellows; if not, good Chablis or white Bordeaux or a dry white California).

Warm: Clean and soaked clams are sauteed in pure butter; when almost done add chopped parsley, fresh small mushrooms, slivered or sliced almonds, a few dices of fresh mild red peppers (or pimientos if your pepper supply is all green at the grocery).

Spoon the finished combination with just a *tiny* drop of Tobasco sauce after the fire is off, well mixed in, onto a piping hot bed of fluffy rice flavored with saffron.

Again, Muscadet, Chablis or another very dry white of your choice.

Please: *don't* use clams from rivers or obviously dirty water. Choose clear, spring-fed lakes where raccoons forage; and *always* clean clams carefully and cook them thoroughly, though not harshly.

7

OFF THE GRILL: ON THE SHORE/ IN THE WOODS

Nothing is so grand as the open grill for shore lunches and woods dinners. Sterno, smokey campfires and hot dogs and bakery buns, half warm canned goods from the market . . . a cheap sad travesty! Lunch in the woods - or *all* the meals in a longer journey in the hinterlands - should match the quality of the hunt and the hunter. Savor and dignity do not disappear when tablecloth and gas stove are far behind. The open grill is the answer. I have not all the secrets. Here are some that will make gourmet delights of nightmares and make you feel you are living in and of the woods and waters - not imposing a cheap civilization upon them! A real sportsman is a king in his domain, a privileged soul. He should eat like one. If you are already a devotee of supermarket charcoal, starter fluid, foil and convenience snacks, don't bother to read this. We're on different wave lengths. You take your path, I'll stick to mine.

1. Always to carry in the hunting car or fishing buggy: 1 box of fine dry maple kindling; shaved maple or cedar for tinder; 1 box of bigger billets of dry maple, thick and chunky; as much bark as you can spare room for in the jeep or wagon; a good grate for a campfire and a good compact self-contained steel barbeque grill with ventilated cover - no fancy stuff with elevator grill and dime-store gadgetry. Honest steel. Finally, a *flame and oven proof* pan, rather shallow, just big enough to fit on top of your smallest grilling surface. Cast iron is perfect - a skillet can do the job.

2. The fire: Build a hot nucleus of very dry tinder and kindling, make a very hot, ardent fire with your dry billets, follow with a layer of rather green maple - gathered in the camp area or carried in - which will calm the fire and make it smoke briefly. Shortly

after this addition, your fire will reach it hottest point. Put the grate on top now so it gets evenly hot in the flames. As soon as flames are almost disappeared you have a super-hot barbeque; slowly the fire will grow less ardent. Unless you cover it, its cooking range - slowly diminishing in temperature - ought to last about 45 minutes to an hour for each 6" or 8" of depth of coals. If you have a lot of cooking to do build the fire thick vertically before putting the grate back on; if you want a cool fire soon, build it thinner up and down. Obviously a deep cast iron barbeque is to be desired. Don't open bottom and side vents more than a bit unless you want a very hot cooking fire for a relatively short period. Hickory or hemlock chipped fine, and a bit wet, adds smokey flavor if you want it but it is very hard to surpass the sugary smoke savor of good northwoods rock maple. Covering the grill partly or completely for one or two minutes drives in smoke flavor but do this *very* cautiously. It is easy to "over smoke" delicate flavors, even with good maple (not to speak of villianous grocery store charcoal whose "savor" resembles diesel engine exhaust).

3. The meat: We assume you are hunters and fishermen and will not be hauling hamburger and hotdogs to camp or cabin. If you must, do such discordant things in suburban backyards.

The secret of grilling is simply to congeal what native albumin you can on the surface, so that juices are driven in, not sucked out by cooking, and then to match meat to fire: simple.

Unless game or fish is marinated in wine, vinegars, or lemon juice - rare in the field or shore situation - it should be liberally rubbed with half a fresh, juicy lemon until every interstice has been "congealed" by the acidic and savorous juice. *Always* carry fresh lemons!

Always carry a good oil - corn, olive or what you prefer. Once rubbed with lemon, brush meat with oil gently and liberally so it is drenched; use your shallow pan and a brush similar to a pastry brush. You can advantageously season your oil with fresh crushed garlic, onions or other spices but be careful *never* to get salt in any form near meat headed for a grill or campfire.

Red meats should be cooked short periods over a very hot fire lighter meats progressively over progressively cooler coals. Thu wild duck, woodcock, venison, and the like want ardent coals, an at the other end of the spectrum all fishes need a cool fire and lon lingering stays on the grill.

All meats should be kept well oiled and only by gently removin the cuts from the grill and resaturating in the shallow pan, then returning to the grill. Don't try haphazard oil-drizzling on the grill itself. You'll waste oil and make smoke. Never use butter until meats are retired to a platter.

All meat should "rest" a bit after grilling; your oven proof and flame proof pan with oily residue from the brushing will, set over the cooling coals, be a perfect "holding" oven.

Always use spatulas for the grill. It is necessary for delicate fish - whole or filleted - and desired for all meat. *Never* puncture broiling meat with a fork: a true disgrace! It is awfully handy to have two broad, stiff spatulas, one with a long handle, one shorter. Fish is turned gently between the two to prevent breaking.

Reliable outdoor grilling takes experience but these ground rules are essential, ensure good results if used with common sense, and imply the outdoors man's ideal: simple, multi-purpose equipment without frills or awkward untransportable variety. Spatulas, pan, grill, fuel; for grocery staples, fresh lemons, oil, seasoning you desire . . . that is about it, the nucleus.

Always remember it is better to have to remove meat to "hold", lift the grill, and refuel the fire, than to use too hot a fire for your meat and burn or dry it. You can always pause but not go back once gone too far, so patience and caution is the rule. Remove the cuts and let the fire cool if you see your cooking go faster than desired.

If you rub red meats with cut or bruised garlic, as many experienced chefs always do before grilling, do this *before* the lemon juice rub. The garlic is especially to be recommended with all venisons, hare, squirrel, and the stronger dark fleshed birds.

4. Top of the grill accompaniments: On an ardent fire: Halves of jumbo onions well drenched with seasoned oil, cut side to fire - skewer with tooth picks to hold them together; wedges or small halves of green or red cabbage; green peppers, halved and well oiled; fresh tomatoes; thin sliced Idaho potatoes (those take little fire-time and will puff up into delicious "souffles");

On slower fires: Thick slices oiled eggplant; split apples, pears, or grapefruit halves (grand for trout breakfasts on frosty spring mornings at streamside camps); sliced onions, preferably thick and cooked not too done; mushrooms if big enough to hold on your grill, or on a finer auxilliary grating put on top of a corner of the barbeque if you have space for this extra piece of cookware;

On almost any fire if watched: Chunks of cauliflower or broccoli tops; small fresh asparagus spears; rather thinly sliced parsnips (cut longwise of course). All can be skewered on "shishkebabs" if you like.

Ingenuity alone limits you. Fresh vegetables on the grill top are a perfect foil to grilled game and, properly, crisply done - never burned or dried out - form a healthful and continually varied accompaniment to wild fresh meat. None require additional vessels or preparation and fit perfectly in the outdoorsman's specification: fast, healthy, balanced, efficient and differently delicious in-the-field meals, centered on game presented at its best amid the woods and waters which produce it.

8

POACHING IN MILK

Pochee au lait - this, a standard and elegant preparation for light delicate meats, takes patience and a certain fussiness since the milk must be hot but must not boil vigorously on direct heat. A double boiler or oven casserole approach is slower but easier and - almost - equivalent in effect. Generally, recall that milk poaching is for "soft" rather than astringent effects. A couple of procedures will suggest principles and other applications.

BASS IN MILK

Heat whole milk short of boiling in a double boiler sauce pan and when hot but not quite scumming transfer to the base boiler where water is boiling merrily. Put in a dash of bruised and rubbed tarragon and add fresh small cuts of boneless bass. Hot milk should just cover pieces of fish. When bass is flaky tender present in a fairly deep, preheated serving dish, add liberal cubes of fresh butter to milky bass, garnish with chopped parsley. This delicate preparation is equally suited to other panfish, whole or in boneless cuts. Walleye filets can be prepared this way but a sufficiently large boiler pan to spread out the bigger filets. If you try it over the fire in a broad pan be very cautious. Beware cooking too fast, scumming and boiling the milk. Mild white ocean fish are equally good so presented.

PHEASANT POCHEE AUX OEUFS

Cut fresh breast of young pheasant in thin slices, poach slowly in milk until done or nearly done. A dash of sweet basil and sage, rubbed fine.

In an oven casserole arrange a bed of fresh peas which have also been slowly and rather lightly cooked in milk with bruised mint leaves. Now arrange poached pheasant over peas, break over, but do not mix in, enough eggs to cover the surface. Don't break the yolks! Add the pheasant poaching milk gingerly around the edges, let the whole "set" together about 40 minutes at most in a docile oven. It may help to butter the casserole dish, but it may not be necessary since the milk is copious. When the whole is fairly solidly set, put lots of butter on top encouraging it to seep down, in and around. Garnish with paprika, serve with a tangy fruit salad and white wine for summer (if you're in France!) or autumn luncheons.

Exactly the same preparation is excellent for ruffed grouse or bob-white quail. The hearty might try this for a pre-hunt breakfast.

9

CULINARY RESCUES

If domestic meat were selected and butchered, transported, kept, abused and cooked as is much game, none would eat it. That is true, especially in America where hunters may too often be careless and ignorant. It is less true in France, never true in Germany; game is too precious, too expensive, too revered. Maybe one day we shall learn. But in any land, in an individual circumstance, the cook will meet a roast that is too old, too tough, too dry, a duck that has flown too long, a pheasant that should have been left to die a patriarch, meats, in a word, which through no one's fault, are going to give a poor impression cooked in usual ways. Usually the culprit will be venison or wild fowl, occasionally a Canada goose but most often a big drake, more rarely upland birds. Too often such meat has not been properly aged (hung) either and has been refrigerated (or worse, frozen!) in its sorry state. Typical American solutions: throw out; give away; marinate too long in something too strong; grind up and combine with something else in sausage or "loaf" or "burger" - the most horrible of all - or simply to mask with strong sauce or spice. There may be a better way, if meat is simply old, dry and tough but wholesome, not spoiled. Here is a "two version" ragout, one for dark, the other for light meat. Whether duck, venison, woodcock, moose, antelope, elk, pheasant, goose, turkey or whatever, cut your boned, defatted, de-gristled "problem" meat into small squares, chips or cubes not larger than 3/4" x 3/4" and proceed as follows in proportion. The result may surprise you!

Red meat ragout
  2 cups cubed raw meat
  1 cup diced turnip
  1 cup diced onion
  ½ cup chopped spinach
  1 bulb garlic, diced
  ½ cup red cabbage shreds
  1 cup red wine vinegar
  Parsley, Laurel , Bay
  1 teaspoon horseradish, dry
  1 teaspoon dry mustard

Light meat ragout
  2 cups cubed raw meat
  1 cup diced turnip
  1 cup diced onion
  ½ cup diced carrots
  ½ bulb garlic, diced
  ½ cup *white* cabbage shreds
  1 cup white wine vinegar
  Parsley, Laurel, Bay
  ½ teaspoon horseradish, dry
  ½ teaspoon dry mustard

Simmer in an oven kettle at 275 degrees or no more than 300 degrees, very tightly covered. Lose as little moisture as possible. Towards 5 hours of cooking things should be extremely tender! Do not stir - do mixing when ingredients are raw and won't break up. About 15 minutes before serving open the pot, drizzle liberally with melted butter, about ½ a quarter stick to this much ragout. Don't stint! Heat briefly to 375 degrees, paprika on top, serve directly onto hot plates over (or side of) fluffy biscuits for light meat ragout, dark, sour rye bread for red.

This rescue operation can turn into a favorite leftover "stew for two" or even a favored entree. As long as approximate proportions are kept it works for any amount of meat. Either formula can be stretched with chopped celery, rutabaga, cauliflower, or even broccoli stems - don't waste tops.

10

FITTING ACCOMPANIMENTS

AIOLI

There are some northern French who think aioli is a garlic flavored mayonnaise liked by southerners. Americans have scarcely heard of it. Apparently no one recalls Alphonse Daudet, describing an autumn of grand chase in the camargue, the strange and wonderful camargue, essence of Provence, of the sea, of the hunt, and proper home of makers and eaters of Aioli. Daudet was fascinated by his evenings in a hut on stilts, home of the guide, the soul of his memory of the camargue. One night the whole evening was spent by the fire, talking of times past, of guns, of game, the host made his aioli. This is a ceremonial as well as a culinary task - the don of the family may count it a privilege. Don't you all remember Daudet's wonderful picture? The camargue is as lovely today - as rich in memory, as in Aioli. The wild horses still roam the meadows, waterfowl teem and a restaurant near the Vaccares still serves, without a blink, savorous boar poached from the government wildlife preserve and so labelled. As Stendhal said, the men of the midi are both brave and frank!

Cloves of huge meridional garlic, white, translucent and mild, were peeled of outer shell - Daudet does not tell us that, but it is still to see, just yesterday, in the cabanas and farm kitchens of Provence - and into a great ceramic mortar such as apothecaries once used to decorate turn of the century windows. Each was crushed lovingly, and the mass, creamy smooth and resplendent with aroma, was worked the evening long. Eventually the crusher began to drip olive oil into his garlic paste without once ceasing the gentle agitation. When evening was done, the aioli was more than half oil, soft as June butter on the table, absolutely uniform in texture, like melted pearls.

Nothing more, nothing less, than these elements - garlic, pure olive oil, much love - make real aioli.

Its savor is enjoyed room temperature, right from the bowl, with raw vegetables cut julienne, as a thin spread for crisp breads, with other spreads on sandwiches and hors d' oeuvres, as a flavoring for sauces, with slices of cold meat and hundreds of other informal "nibble worthy" tidbits.

Hot, it is spread on thick slices of French bread to be toasted over the open grill, or daubed on servings of roast meat; a marvellous warm (not hot) hors d' oeuvre is made by cutting thin rounds of

THE CORNCRAKE

French bread and crisping them in a hot oven with slices of light cheese on top to melt, topping these to serve with warm aioli and great golden walnut halves.

In many a provincial country manse, dessert following the main meal will consist of a bowl of walnuts, aioli at room temperature to spread on, or dip into with, the halved nuts, several cheeses and wine.

For hot uses where texture is less noticed, tolerable aioli can be made in a blender or food processor, but the old way alone makes the best result. Only large white garlics are mild enough for this dish. It is definitely not worth making only with the small violet Louisiana garlic sold in some stores. The giant white California "elephant" garlic is a near approximation   if not a duplicate, of real southern French or Spanish garlic.   Don't make much at a time, and always keep at room temperature.   Use sparingly until you adjust your taste buds to real food!

MUSHROOMS PUREE

Divide a large harvest of fresh northern mushrooms - buttons or morels - into the most perfect and large, and the others. Wash and lightly steam the less perfect and the pieces, dice fine, and reduce to a creamy puree in an electric blender using a few tablespoons of melted butter as liquid. Finish cooking the puree gently in a medium oven adding at the end an egg yolk and a tiny bit of fresh cream to give a rich texture - about one yolk and one tablespoon of cream to each 2 cups of puree, more if you wish it very rich.

Saute the remaining mushrooms gently in butter keeping them whole and presentable, and add drained water chestnuts, split in half and quartered walnuts, about ¼ cup of each to each cup of mushrooms. When the mushrooms are tender but not overcooked, present the dish in one of three ways:

a) Pour puree from oven dish into skillet and serve directly to the table, over crisp grilled or toasted French bread;

b) Combine the puree and mushroom/nut/chestnut mixtures in individual ramekins lined with buttered well cooked leaves of spinach and serve piping hot;

c) Put the two mixtures together, fill small pates or even tarts with them (excellent hors d' oeuvres), bake briefly in a hot oven and dust the tops with paprika. It is also possible to bake this mixture in a larger pie shell; if you do this saute the large mushrooms and chestnuts more lightly and make your puree thicker (extra egg yolk) to achieve a more compact servable result.

This "essence" of mushroom flavor should not be masked by other strong spices or more salt than is in the butter and the crusts if used. An ideal accompaniment to fish, light meats, or for luncheon alone, with white wine and crisp early summer salad greens.

WILD ASPARAGUS

Asparagus, wild, feral or domestic, if very slender and extremely fresh is a marvellous salad green. The tender tops should when possible be reserved for use raw in this most superb of summer salads - fit for kings. Larger asparagus, or a bountiful harvest tempts one to cook the vegetable as a foil for fish or fowl and especially in summer (in Wisconsin) the former.

To go with a rather rich or creamy fish preparation, simply saute tender fresh asparagus tops in butter and when not too done squeeze fresh lemons into the butter in the pan to make a lemon butter in which to present the vegetable.

With a simply astringent broiled trout or bass, itself well drizzled in butter and lemon, use this richer preparation: Divide asparagus into tops and tougher lower parts. Steam these last rather well and puree in an electric blender until smooth. Blend heavy cream and a tiny bit of rubbed sage into the puree while still in the blender, then simmer gently in an oven proof casserole. Steam the asparagus tops very lightly, leaving them crisp and dark green. Put these in a hot serving dish, top liberally with butter and a dash of coarse fresh pepper, top with the puree sauce and garnish with golden toasted fine crumbs of French bread thoroughly dried and drizzled with fresh butter melted softly: Gold dust on a green carpet, as gorgeous as it is flavorful, intensely asparagus, accented not masked. Sprigs of fresh parsley on the edges of the server will highlight the green tone.

Exactly the same preparation is effective with fresh broccoli but both parts of this vegetable require a bit longer steam cooking than asparagus - particularly so the bottom stalks of broccoli which can be rather fibrous.

QUICK DARK BREAD (BISCUITS)

Dissolve a half a large cake compressed yeast in 1¾ cups of *warm* water in a *warm* crockery bowl; add 1½ cups *Millers' bran,* just as it comes from the sack - not a cereal from a box! Finish working in stone ground whole wheat flour until you have a light dough, almost sticky, just *barely* dry enough to work. Knead on a floured board until elastic and springy; sprinkle in a little cider vinegar as you work. Don't add too much flour - scrape your board frequently; divide into golf ball sized rolls, cover each thoroughly with flour and pack gently into a shallow pan, floured not greased. Let rise 60 - 70 minutes in a closed oven with a pan of piping hot water for moist heat. These nuggets will not rise too much, don't expect it. Bake at 350 degrees for about 30 minutes, until tapping the tops makes a hollow sound and until the smell is irresistible. Serve hot with big bowls of *Bouilli.* The buns should break apart, be soft and chewy with a lightly crusty exterior, and keep a day at most. Gently rewarm leftovers in moist heat. Try adding a bit of sage or thyme, tarragon or oregano for variety.

PATEE DE FOIE SAUVAGE

(One may add hearts and gizzards of grouse, pheasant quail and partridge to these preparations but they should be lightly par boiled *first* because they require more cooking; livers are never par boiled!

Saute fresh livers of game birds quite well done in a skillet with butter, finely chopped onion, garlic, parsley, oregano and thyme, just a touch of the last two. Drain and grind or chop very fine. Mix with finely chopped ripe olives in the proportion 1 to 4, olives to liver. Reserve pan drippings.

Cut dry French bread thin (¼") and into 3" squares; edges resulting from this are crushed into fine crumbs and toasted golden brown in an oven pan.

Mix liver, crumbs, pan drippings into a firm paste, since the olives are oily you may not need all the drippings. Put a generous layer of the paste on each square of bread and top with a thin coat of grated romano cheese staying judiciously in from the edges. Toast in a fairly hot oven until the cheese is melted and starting to brown at the thin edges of the topping. Garnish with paprika. Serve as a *hot hors-d' oeuvre,* or with a large green luncheon salad.

PATE FOID

For a cold variation proceed as above but use less of the pan drippings in order to get a thicker pate and add about as much finely crumbled hard cooked egg yolk as olives. Omit any cheese, chill and serve as a spread with French bread hot from the oven (or preferably grill) which you have moistened liberally with those pan drippings not used in the pate.

"GNOCCI" A LA FOIE

Mix equal parts cold mashed potato, chopped sauteed liver, crumbs and grated romano cheese, link into a stiff paste with beaten egg yolk; roll in balls, chill, roll in crumbs, chill again and fry gently, fresh from the ice box, in garlic butter; drain well, dry in warm oven on a grill if necessary for crispness. Serve hot with soup or salad course or as a hot *hors d' oeuvre.*

CHEESE PANCAKES WITH VARIATIONS

The skillet baked cake is not merely a pleasant breakfast bread or cereal substitute. Flavored with cheese and meat and meat spices it makes a superb luncheon staple or a potato/pasta substitute with game main dishes.

Start with a hearty formula, omit sugar and use buttermilk, sour cream or creamed cottage or ricotta cheese instead of milk or sweet cream. Our favorite is built around this base:

1 cup flour;

2 egg whites beaten stiff as if for meringue; set aside;

3 egg yolks;

¼ stick soft butter, salt and pepper in minute quantity;

1 small cake baker's **ye**ast, whif of sugar, *not* more;

just enough sour cream to make a very thick doughy "molassassy" mix. Allow to rest and develop in a bowl near the stove and start with room temperature ingredients to flavor yeast development.

Before baking fold in the stiff egg whites and one of the following "fillings":

a) diced smoked ham;

b) chopped deer or game bird liver, precooked of course

c) coarsely diced cheddar or swiss cheese;

d) grated romano and parmesan cheeses with finely diced onion and green pepper

e) combination of a) and c) or a) and d).

Bake slowly on a buttered griddle, turning as often as necessary to produce an even, golden pancake. The result should be fluffy and thick. For careful cooking keep diameters about 4" to 4½".

Sour cream makes a medium thick batter; buttermilk thinner, cottage or ricotta cheese a thicker batter. If you need more liquidity use plain sweet milk to dilute cottage or ricotta cheeses.

FRUIT SALAD AND DRESSING

Cubed into a shell of bib lettuce in a cold dish: oranges, apples, watermelon balls, honeydew melon balls, very ripe pineapple, juliennes of avocado flesh, halved almonds and walnuts, pear, nectarine and strawberries for color. Dress with half and half mayonnaise, whipping cream, rubbed mint and a dash of lime juice gently mixed and spooned over finished individual salads. Garnish with wedged lemon and lime. Fresh native berries can be added.

NATIVE GREEN SUMMER SALAD

Toss fresh clean greens from the marsh marigold cut coarsely with watercress and chopped raw wild asparagus; if possible add a large proportion of chopped cooked native mushrooms, drained and chilled. Fresh coarse ground white pepper straight from the grinder and red wine vinegar and oil in cruets finish this simple but elegant "great lakes" salad. It may be tricky to get these ingredients together but it can be done. Try to schedule your guests to fit such happy coincidences. This is a perfect foil for a grand preparation of an early season muskellunge, or elegant fresh broiled rainbow trout. If your main dish is more ordinary you might wish to garnish your salad with strips "julienne" of smoked pickled venison.

SMOKED FISH SALAD

Bass, muskellunge or any easily boned fresh game fish can be rubbed with lemon juice *(fresh please)* and *slowly* maple smoked in a small smoker. The well done smoked fish should be loosely flaked up with a dinner fork, tossed with equal quantities of chopped parsley, celery, green pepper and coated with a creamy dressing made of approximately equal parts of good egg mayonnaise, sour thick cream and buttermilk, a squirt or so of fresh lemon juice, a pinch each of thyme, oregano and sage, finely rubbed. This can be used in hollow tomatoes, for open (or conventional) salad sandwiches, or any other use for which shrimp, salmon or tuna salads might be employed.

FROZEN DESSERTS

Here are three superbly sinful ice cream variations to be made with native products - desserts forming noteworthy postludes to dinners and luncheons which celebrate the sublime quality of native fish and game when prepared with affection and care.

The basis of all of these is rich French vanilla ice cream. If you make your own, so much the better. If you buy your product *please* make it *true* French vanilla, rich with egg and cream. Grocery store ice creams are usually horrible concoctions unworthy of a carefully prepared table!

Melt a pint of French vanilla ice cream to creamy texture.

Coarsely crack into chunks a cup or slightly more of Wisconsin wild hazel nuts, well dried; toast lightly in a medium oven. Mix into the melted ice cream with a pinch of cardamon (powdered) and ¼ cup of real Wisconsin or Vermont maple syrup, with about 2 table-spoons of cognac. Refreeze in individual parfait glasses.

Variation: thoroughly mix into melted ice cream enough dutch cocoa powder to create a dark chocolate color, darker than most commercial chocolate ice creams; add toasted hazel nuts as above, plus a bit less than ¼ cup of white creme de cocoa. Refreeze and serve in similar parfait glasses. This may be happily topped with home whipped cream into which you have blended enough creme de menthe to create a sharp green hue and a refreshing mint flavor.

Variation: add a cup per pint of Juneberries (service berries) wild blueberries or wild blackberries, which have "aged" at room temperature several days to mature their flavor. Cognac and a pinch of nutmeg well mixed in are optional highlights. Refreeze and serve as above.

11

RECIPES FROM SOUTHERN ITALY

A geographically invisible line, from Terracine on the Tyrrhenian Sea to Termoli on the Adriatique, marks a frontier which has perhaps never been crossed safely at the time of the Longobards: for eleven centuries it determined the destiny of the Italian peninsula. Open to influences from Spain, North Africa, Greece and the Holy Land, southern Italy is deprived of the economic and cultural unity which distinguishes the center and the north.

Pouilles, largest of the four southern regions possesses the least varied relief, the fewest contrasts. The plain called "Tavoliere" (table) spreads beyond mount Gargano, fertile in legumes, olive and almond groves, cerals and vineyards, the most productive of southern Italy. The natural bridge between Eastern Europe and the orient, Bruidisi was the naval base of the Romans and crusaders alike. Until yesterday, it was the "packing point" for West Indies bound travellers. Tarente, founded allegedly in B.C. 708 by Taras, son of Neptune, was a naval power, the Paris of the Graeco-Latin world, where Greek and Roman cultures fused to form western civilization. Lecca, wrote Gregorovius, was the "Florence of the Baroque".

All aspects of the life of Pouilles are the result of this historical kaleidoscope, which explains as well the particularities of apulien cuisine.

The "ragu' " apulien, as baroque as Lecca's decor, is the fruit of just as lively a fantasy. A skillet of hot fat, chopped onions and basil plus a whole fistful of aromatics - clove, fennel, fenugreek as well as almost any similar spices available, ginger and red pepper included, is prepared and a boned portion of mutton or venison is set to cook over slow heat. When half done it is smothered in an old red wine and left to simmer almost infinitely. Just before serving a puree of fresh tomatoes is added to the nearly dehydrated pan drippings. Serving is in shallow tureens, with a robust red Trani wine.

The glory of the region is "orata alla pugliese". Designed around the native Daurade, this plan can be used with any 2 - 3 pound gamefish. For six persons choose a generous fish, about 1/8 pound of real Italian Pecorino cheese if you can find it, grated, six small potatoes, three bulbs of garlic (always lime sized white garlic in the south) parsley and about 8 ounces of olive oil. Garlic and parsley are chopped fine, bathed in oil, potatoes cut in slices. In a flat casserole chopped greens, potatoes and cheese - half precisely of each - are arranged in a bed. The cleaned fish sleeps here; the remainder of greens, potatoes, then cheese form his coverlet. After 45 minutes to an hour at medium heat a royal feast begins. Be sure the fish himself is well done, warns the cook. Apulien ovens bake slowly but lovingly, burning stubs of grapevines (sarments) and almond wood.

The first of these specialties is well suited to unmarinated cuts of young venison - corn fed Portage county spike bucks. Don't attempt it with old north country lunkers. "Orata alla pugliese" is successful with big bass or well fattened fall walleyes. The "portions for six", of course, assumes a huge salad, appetizer and pasta and/or rice on the side, wine (usually the exquisite white Locorotondo of the region) and a final course of cheese, fruit, nuts and a sweeter wine. Under more "American" circumstances plan it for three - or even two! Since you will never see Locorotondo outside Italy substitute a very light Italian white wine of your choice, or even Muscadet if it is young. White bordeaux is a big but not a bad choice.

12

A SIMPLE REPAST

Even Paris has changed. Les Halles are no more - the market - basket of civilization, the legend, lives only in fantastic memories. Commemorated by luminous pictures in literature and a couple of real idioms and phrases in current French. Rue coquillieres is still there, along side the giant hole where the city of Paris is rebuilding a park and various other projects yet undefined on the site of the old market where draymen once shouted in humid Parisian dawn. Some very posh restaurants still spread their tables and banks of sea food and salad on the narrow sidewalk, a meter short of grumbling bull - dozers, and Saint Eustache slumbers still in all her decadent gothic magnificence, haunting a scene which too much resembles Gehenna, one would think, for the aesthetic ease of her guardian angel.

Just a block west, hidden around a narrow corner, is Dehellevin, point of pilgrimmage, a corner building housing the worlds most famous and certainly largest selection of gourmet cooking para- phernalia. For more than half a century, all the great restaurants, clubs, hotels, and gourmet cooks, private and otherwise, have sup- plied themselves from this source. From Moscow to Tokyo, Cape- town to Trondheim near the pole, cooks and hotels turn to Deheller- in. Your pastry in Austria like your omelette in Rhiems or your ris- taffel in New Dehli is cooked and likely served in and on equipment which came from this little haunted corner of the city of light. There is no piece of cooking, preparing or serving equipment ap- propriate to anyone's grand cuisine not there in stock, in every size from minute to gargantuan. No lover of cuisine can fail to make this call, amid the ruins of what was once the world's most mind boggling market place for fine food.

I recall well my first visit, one luscious sun bathed late October afternoon. I was so busy making notes a wonderful little old lady mistook me for a clerk, and drawing her scarcely five foot height to full stature, asked me to find her a certain tiny pastry form she could not do without for the events of that very evening. At least I knew I looked Parisian!

We had walked to downtown Paris all the way from home near Bois de Vincennes. What a spectacle!

Through one little community after another, for every ten stores six are groceries, bakeries, wine shops, cafes, fruit stands or other vendors of food. Food and drink are everywhere. There is almost no refrigeration, fruits and vegetables are fresh, ripe, perfect, of a variety and quality and freshness simply incomprehensible in America. Prices are absurdly low, as low as restaurants tend now to be exorbitant.

In October stores and the big outdoor markets are exploding with fresh game, in fur and feathers, resplendent brilliances of pheasants, irridescent blues and greens of rank upon rank of ducks, grey and red partridge, fat French woodcock, becassines (snipe), hares and rabbits only to mention the most common. Paris love and revere their game, preparing it with exquisite care and economy. (Big game is less common in Paris markets - in Dauphine , for example, one sees whole unskinned deer - chevreuil - hanging in butcher shops; each customers' preference is cut from the deer until it simply vanishes and is replaced by another.) In spite of all this cuisine at fingers' range Parisians like most French are thin, active, extremely fast and habitual walkers, rarely fat and wheel bound. Encouraging. Fast or convenience foods are rare. Good stores simply do not have prepared junk food. Everything is *real* - fresh, true, honest. Vast truck loads of spring water and wine beyond belief replace the American pop binge (a litre of superb "vin ordinaire" costs 40 cents to 60 cents in most cities!). I love to watch whole truck loads of garlic being carted into a market, in the rosy dawn. By evening it will all be gone, along with the pheasants, ducks, onions and all the rest. All this I say to celebrate my prejudice and illustrate the nature of my tastes. This is a civilization on the Mediterranean model - for civilized men who live to eat, and for all the finest little day by day glories of a marvellous world. We have everything to learn.

We left Dehellerin hungry. Who could not? It conjured a fantastic reminiscence of every fabulous gourmet delight ever enjoyed. We stopped in the tiny Darne shop near the Theatre Francais, amid the slightly intoxicating perfumes of oil, wood, leather, and saddle soap, dimly, warmly lit by afternoon sun sparkling in silver plate, engraving on fire brilliant steel and the glow of rubbed walnut, to dream and heft trim doubles, fine as violins, and more expensive; the cocker spaniel ears of Darne's famous profile, the "fusil juxtapose a canon fixe" sprout everywhere, from packed racks. Visions of pheasants rising before panther-rapid barrels in a perfect gilded afternoon in fields old before Columbus sailed, crowd with almost painful urgency. Two fine old gentlemen are talking guns in a dark corner, recalling the days of youth. But what could be finer than all this? Stuffed ducks beckon from the rafters.

On the other side of the Seine the gastronomic emergency is given first aid, if not a cure, with fresh roasted chestnuts and generous glasses of red cotes du Rhone in a quaintly tiny cafe presided over by a generous madame who mistakes us for Quebecois because of my accent. For an American, this is a compliment! Parisians are ticklish for *their* French - which is different from anyone else's.

What better than to describe a dinner, a late, evening long regalis, the celebration a bourgeois Parisian of the finery that haunts our tongues at each moment of each day spent in this fairly heavenly wonderland? Only dinners like this make it possible to get through the streets and aromas of any French city and actually do any work. Distraction is overpowering, even so.

The sun is almost set now, casting golden luminous glows along streets of Isle Saint Louis and Cite where the traces of Roman walls are still visible behind the courts and main sidewalks. Like most Paris apartments, our hosts is old, grand, rich with wood, and from the inside almost chateau-like. (Nothing on the exterior, by the way, would encourage such expectations! Quite the reverse! But one needs faith - and it is always rewarded in this land of surprises and contrasts.)

M. and M. Regnier are comfortable middle class Parisians, and there is little attempt to obey to standards of etiquette in small private gatherings. Without further ado we were admitted to the small kitchen from which elegant odors were rising. In the panelled book lined parlor, meanwhile, a simple buffet was put up in a sort of belle epoque still life, Darnes and a fabulous 2 kilo 20 gauge Baby Breton peeked from a high rack, wine glasses sparkled and old leather bindings caught the last copper rays of sun streaming through the croisillons of a bay which glimpsed the Seine and the skyline of Rivedroit.

Squares of neatly cut fish had just been popped in a skillet of butter, basil and fine chopped shallots. Mrs. Regnier was sauteeing them gently, using a wooden spatula. She broke not one cube. A double boiler on the back of the range was ready to receive the lightly browned cubes of pink-white fish, and while she fussed over pates ready to bake in neat forms (from Dehellerin, of course!) clustered on a tiny work table. Cream, egg yolk, a whiff of flour in the skillet, gently adjusted with the wooden spatula until a thick creamy yellow sauce resulted, and then a dash of courvoisier cognac. Sauce in the double boiler, skillet wiped carefully clean, all in apparent twinklings. While the skillet rested on the stove before another careful "cleaning out" with a trifle of oil, the shells were filled with the bisque of fish, a few niblets of fresh blood red raw tomato in each shell, a few crumbs on top and into the ancient gas fired oven to bake, along with a pan of fresh noisettes (hazelnuts) - appetite teasers.

Now a pot boiling ever so gently on the back burner is brought up. Barely covered with a broth, which started as water, seasoned with rosemary, fennel, laurel and a few garlic cloves crushed, were ten exquisite becassines. They were virtually done now, and Mrs. Regnier now heated more butter in her purified skillet and gradually she browned her little snipe and put them in a casserole. When all were gilded the broth went into the skillet butter and the result cooked down to about half volume. Then just a triffle of white chablis, over the becassines in the casserole, and the whole into the oven. By a miracle so typically French and feminine, the fish was done, and the new tenant had plenty of space and a lower temperature - mainly achieved by putting a slender block of wood in the oven door! No thermometers for Mrs. Regnier!

While the pates settled Madame tossed a darkly verdant salad of leeks (the French poivron) neatly chopped, shredded leaf lettuce, watercress, a few diced radishes and gorgeous tomato wedges. Lime and lemon slices around the edge and accompanying cruets of red wine vinegar and Italian olive oil - that is all. This went to the buffet in Mrs. Regnier's steady hands, pates followed, with our hostess while a bottle of green-gold Muscadet came lightly chilled from an old wooden crate full of craggy ice chunks which had been hiding under the sink. Salad and French bread, fresh and crisp from the most favored boulauger of Ile Saint Louis, came next. Muscadet, the fish wine par excellence, is a fairly common treat in Paris, but any that reaches the United States is likely to be too old to measure to standard.

Then a bit of Perrier water to "cleanse the palate", and out came the casserole of snipe and a bottle of old bordeaux from the cupboard ledge where, uncorked, it had been enticingly resting on a little silver plate. Utter simplicity. Dessert was a common wooden bowl of apples, pears, huge Italian grapes, silver compotes of shelled almonds, and individual half golden melons lightly sprinkled with brandy. A plate of cheeses and another bottle - for a special occasion - sparkling Italian Asti Spumanti, better than champagne, the storied "nebieux" of the "Charterhouse of Parma."

This meal was utterly simple, really economical and interrupted the sociability of the evening not at all. It was a part of the celebration of friendship, a sort of model of provincial simplicity interpreted in a Parisian setting. I think of it as a perfect synthesis of love and casualness, the essence of the *real* cooking ethic, the one *a propos* to great game and generous souls. The Regniers, I'm told, also gave some very distinguished dinners, more in the Paris mode. I'm just as glad that I was too unimportant to be at such occasions; they could not have been so gay and we could scarcely have crashed the kitchen!

13

AN EVENING AT OLD TAMARACK LODGE

I recall in particular an evening at the club when the old guard was in full regalia: the conferees of Old Tamarack were back from the first long week at their hideaway, and in town "uncle" Bert had been entertaining a visiting professor from Montpellier, in the heart of Provence - a guest who (like most of Bert's friends) was a gourmet almost before he was a scholar. They had been hunting and the men of Old Tamarack had been hunting and manning Musky tackle and the little bass boat in October sunsets. "Uncle" Bert called up a magnificent party to close his friend's visit, a typical last evening fete, the proper crown to a week at a hunting chateau in Normandy translated as only "Uncle" Bert could, into a jolly American synthesis. Naturally the only site for such a regalia was the good club, with it's wondrous beamed halls and last century elegance - not to speak of a magnificent kitchen full of French brass ware, grand wood burning ranges and an open pit barbeque, a kitchen where Bert could play at cuisine and personally fuss over each detail of a dinner. He was a little boy at heart, it all came out in the kitchen.

The scenes of that evening remind me of Alphonse Daudet's ecstatic painting of the gay Christmas eve feast in a medieval chateau, the anticipation of which led an unfortunate abbe' down Mephisto's primrose path. Do you recall *Les Trois Messes Basses*? I have always sympathized with the poor weak gourmand!

Flickering lamps, roaring fire, luminescent glassware, golden and ruby torches which were carafes of wine on candle and lantern lit tables, jewel like silverware - all was a jewelled fairyland. And the smells, the aromas - one could blame no hurried preacher who swallowed his ordinary and slurred his offices with such visions dancing in his head. The club this night was at its best!

Waiters with trays of glasses, rich orange red manhattans, frosty, ice veiled martinis, chablis and champagne cocktails, circulated as did others with carts of hors d' oeuvres: pates of grouse and pheasant liver, delicate juliennes of smoked-pickled venison, smoked northern bass, brushed with butter, presented on crisp lettuce with wedges of lemon - and so many more. Rich split pea soup made with salt pork stock alternated with a dark rich soup of long simmered bone carcasses of rabbit, grouse, pheasant, squirrel and duck, the meat from which had gone into Bert's various gourmet creations. Richly reduced, laced with onion, garlic, carrots, dried beans and laurel, this dark thick soup didn't steam, it fairly smouldered in silver tureens. Later the chef told me Bert started his soup exactly one week before the party. It had never stopped simmering. That a Frenchman could glory in!

There were several regular roasted birds on platters on the grand buffet before the fire - duck, pheasant, grouse, each with conventional sage stuffing of bread croutons, celery, onion, sage, chopped giblets, nuts, mushrooms; but there were mixed bag creations also, which stick in my mind. One was a huge mound of smartly curried rice with four casseroles around it on chafing dishes: sauteed Wisconsin River ducks, rich with slivered almonds and cointreau and the pan butter; grouse in a buttery sweet cream fricasse sauce with spanish sherry in which they had simmered all afternoon; pheasant breasts poached in white chablis and tarragon, and finally a simple omelette in little squares liberally filled with chopped walnuts and diced woodcock lightly sauteed in olive oil, garlic and sage, and diced green peppers. This was served like a conventional Dutch Indies "ristaffel" - a bit of each of the boneless sauced birds around a mound of curried rice in the center of your plate: what a heady congregation!

A similar ristaffel next door on the buffet featured a milder rice, yellow with saffron, and casseroles of crisp breaded and sauteed bite size cuts of panfish, of muskellunge slowly baked in a sour cream, butter and wine sauce, and of broiled bass in lime - butter - a delightful variation.

Equally memorable was a provincial skillet piled with bits of muskellunge meat, bass, walleyed pike and lake trout lightly sauteed in olive oil with wedges of tomato, onion, cloves of garlic and chopped green pepper, seasoned with lemon juice, fennel, dill seed, thyme, laurel and sage. Utterly simple but delicious. The professor from Montpellier must have felt most at home.

All these combinations swim in my memory and create jolly thoughts of what to do with autumn's mixed rewards. All were simple juxtapositions, supple and making the most of natural differences and subtle savours.

Bert's dinner was as always a success. So much so that a couple of years later his colleague hosted a similar bounty at an exclusive Marseille cafe' in the ancient, Greek-settled Mediterranean city where both were attending a conference. I suspect Bert was more than repaid for his week long preparation and the bill they must have sent him.

I enjoyed it all as a guest, young and impressionable. I have been improvising on these ideas ever since. There were no recipes, Bert did it with nose, tasting and a keen "feel." He loved good things, revered wild foods, and his love and quiet care, rather than any haughty precision, showed in all his gourmand wanderings. Maybe that was his best legacy as a man of cheer, good company, and true generosity.

14

SPORT HUNTING IN FRANCE

The number of French hunters has, since the war, grown just apace with the general population. Considering the increasing urbanization of France, this shows substantial interest in shooting sports. France has more open space than most European nations; average population density of 86 per square kilometer.

As in the U.S., separate firearms regulations for big game attempt to encourage humane harvest and prevent waste. Since 1972 it has been illegal to fire on game beyond 300 meters distant (mountain hunting is particularly in mind here) or to carry an arm with sighting equipment allowing ranges beyond 300 meters. Conventional prohibitions against shooting larger game with inadequate calibers are routine, also.

Sangliers, or wild boar, are in a special class so far as big game desireability is concerned. Wild populations are increasingly limited but preserve raising of boar (as *gibier d'elevage)* is being attempted with success. The Sanglier is often hunted with slug loads in a bird gun, and is considered a major trophy, as well as a culinary delicacy. The story is told of village hotels in the wild and independent Camargue whose menus still frankly advertise wild boar poached from the federal game preserve nearby.

Feathered game (besides the extremely popular *lievre,* or hare, and rabbit) whether stocked *(gibier d'elevage)* or natural, is France's chief glory, has been so for some time, and will remain so in the forseeable future.

Much of France is agricultural, a mixture of lowland, pools and ponds, cropland, woodlots, windrows and streams, offering substantial habitat for woodcock, snipe, shorebirds, doves, pigeons *(ramiers* or *palombes),* quail, red and grey partridge, and pheasants pursued by French shotgunners. Quail, partridge, lievre, lapin and pheasant, particularly the latter, may be *gibier d 'elevage,* released annually by restocking programs of the *Associations Communales de Chasse agreees,* as well as private owners and the few U.S. variety game preserves. In spite of environmental pressures, native gamebirds are in good condition in most areas. On the typical Association hunt the shooters (who are often owners of some part or even all of the land administered and managed by the Association) may be shooting both natural and stocked game birds.

The long traditional seasons and (except for the *Plan de Chasse* on big game) lack of bag limits have drawn attention away from other sources of game scarcity, mainly dwindling habitat; pressure relieving measures for Europe's migratory birds remind the French that similar measures would be workable for their beloved *piece de resistance,* the native hare, rabbit, partridge and pheasant.

Some knowledgeable authorities believe artificially raised ducks may be the *gibier d 'elevage* of the future as pheasant strains show disease problems, and native birds fall under increasing pressure habitat as well as gun-wise.

France is on the flyway of enormous numbers of waterfowl which migrate from nesting grounds in northern Europe. Waterfowl hunting is spotty more because of local stopover conditions than a lack of birds flying over. The capitol of waterfowling is probably the fabulous Camargue, in southern France, comprising vast brackish marshes around the mouth of the Rhone below Arles in Provence, but excellent shooting is had on marshes from one end of France to the other, in good years. Naturally not every Frenchman has such habitats within reach, geographically or financially, but marsh gunning is extremely popular.

Thrushes are still shot in France, largely on passes. This practice is frowned upon by some European gunners (and some in France) but the little birds are table worthy and are probably the only flying game easily available to some shooters who cannot find the means to join an Association managing a variety of upland game. They are not an easy target.

The *grand tetras,* or *grand coq de bruyere,* is sought by few French hunters since its range is limited in extent. It is a special challenge and a contrast with other upland birds. Hunted during its characteristic spring territorial display (cocks only) it is a large flamboyant grouse, also known as the black grouse or black cock. The spring hunt follows central and eastern European tradition; elsewhere it is also hunted in autumn over pointing dogs. As with other grouse, harvesting displaying males is consistent with sustained production.

The *Becasse,* or European woodcock, is a somewhat larger bird than our own *philohela minor,* but one equally loved and sought in France by avid specialists as well as casual uplanders. It is a difficult target and a delicacy. The common snipe, or *Becassine,* sometimes affectionately called *princesse du marais,* is probably more popular than its state-side counterpart, and is also a challenging target. The flight of these gamebirds is a paradigm for all tricky shots on feathered game: the quail which finally abandons its typical straightaway flight on third flush is likened to *"le plus vicieuse des becassines!"*

Wild game is sold freely in France - indeed it is imported from other countries for butcher shops. Game shot in large organized shoots may be sold ultimately other than to those who reduce it to possession, though most individual sportsmen use the game they kill personally. Generally, on the few commercial preserves the eventual cost of game (usually pheasant and hare) approximates or exceeds the retail market value, except for extremely proficient (lucky?) shooters.

In spite of legislative, economic and law enforcement problems, the French hunting establishment offers desireable examples to some other progressive Europeans. In a recent interview the president of the Royal St. Hubert Club of Belgium could point with envy to the revenues the French return to resource protection from license fees (66% overall), the number and quality of Federal game protectors, and the institution and success of the *plan de chasse* for large game - all serious advances on the current situation in Belgium, the Low Countries, and Luxembourg (signers of the 1972 Benelux Convention for improvement of game and hunting conditions). Obviously her position in the Continental community is an incentive for France to succeed in improving her resources.

There is no need to reiterate that the Frenchman likes his shotgun in 12 or 16 gauge, in side by side *(juxtapose')* or superposed *(superpose')* formation. And, the French are very much shotgunners, both by circumstance (concentration of activity on feathered and small game and comparatively scattered supplies of large game) and preference. Indeed, the *petoire,* (which means the gentleman's shotgun, literally a 'popgun') is almost synonymous with sporting arm in much of France. The French themselves make excellent double guns and the French gunner can choose among a vast array of Continental, Nipponese and American examples of the art. Magazine shotguns of Belgian Browning manufacture, as well as those of Manufrance of St. Etienne are quite common, particularly for waterfowl hunting. Repeaters are not by any means looked down upon as, for example, they are in the British Isles and some other European nations. They are not, however, the common choice of any great contingent of shooters.

Lines of major U.S. arms are available in France, from such *armuriers* as Kerne, with huge showroom stocks in Versailles and central Paris. American advertising of sporting arms in France is comparatively light.

Rifles of military caliber and configuration are illegal in France (though many may here and there be kept and used, often relics of the French resistance), and sporting rifles are common only in areas where big game is reasonably accessible. The typical weapon of the *garde chasse* is a side by side 12 gauge bored *lisse* and *choke,* to use the terms of convention.

THE HARE